Tongue of
Flame

Tongue of Flame

THE LIFE OF

LYDIA MARIA CHILD

Milton Meltzer

Thomas Y. Crowell

New York

Acknowledgments

The chief source for this book is Lydia Maria Child's own writing—books and articles—and most importantly her own correspondence. About 175 of her letters were published a few years after her death. But over a thousand more are still unpublished. I am deeply indebted to the following for permission to use excerpts from many of the unpublished letters of Mrs. Child in their possession: The Women's Archives, Radcliffe College; The Houghton Library, Harvard University; Cornell University Library; Massachusetts Historical Society; Boston Public Library; American Antiquarian Society; New York Public Library; New York Historical Society; William L. Clements Library, University of Michigan; Yale University Library; Friends Historical Library of Swarthmore College; The Ohio Historical Society.

Many thanks are due the librarians of these institutions for their patience with me and for their useful suggestions in tracking down manuscript material, and to the librarians of the Schomburg Collection of the New York Public Library and the New York Historical Society for access to nineteenth-century newspaper and pamphlet files.

The author is especially grateful to Mrs. Arthur Cort Holden of New York. Her enthusiasm for any attempt to rediscover our American heritage, and particularly the magnificent part played by many women in creating it, was a constant stimulus to this writer. Her generous loan of rare source material from her private library on women made the task both easier and more enjoyable.

Finally, I want to thank Hilda Meltzer for her encouragement, Amy Meltzer for her criticism, and Anne Grandinetti for typing the final manuscript.

CONTENTS

1 ɨɨ A Fugitive Slave

Maria was sitting on a tall barrel of crackers where her father's arms had swung her to get her out of the way. She stretched overhead to reach the towel on the nail and tossed it to her father. Mr. Francis mopped the sweat from his face, ruddy and glistening from the heat of the big ovens. Then he hoisted the big mug of ale to his mouth and tilted his head back for a long, cooling swallow.

Maria waited patiently. Maybe this time he would feel like talking to her a little. She liked playing around the busy bakery, even though her father complained she slowed things down. Anyhow, she could always be sure of Convers. Her brother was fourteen now—he was six years older than Maria—but he put in many long hours helping out his father every day. She could talk to Convers. He didn't think an eight-year-old was beneath notice, and besides, he could test what he was learning by trying it out on her. Most of what he recited out of the books he was studying didn't mean much to Maria. But she liked to hear the rhythm and the music of the lines and she would play with the strange new words, weaving them into nonsense rhymes or stringing them together into sentences that almost seemed to make sense.

Everyone in the family respected Convers. This passion for books he had shown so early was a surprise, but a pleasure, too. Mr. Francis was fascinated by his unusual son—named after himself—and patient with him. He had decided Convers would have the chance to go to college. Maria wished her father would find the time to sit quietly and talk with her, too. He rarely did at home, even at table or at bedtime. Oh, he would tumble her about once in a while, and then she loved to be wrapped in that sweet, warm smell of the bakery that always clung to him. But she was the baby of the large family, after all, and with eight to ten people always about the house, plus innumerable aunts and uncles, she usually felt left out. That was why she would stop at the bakery on the way home from school, or play there for hours during the long summer days. Not only to see Convers, but hoping for a lucky moment when she might find her father pausing between his chores.

It was from his slow and infrequent words that she had stitched together her picture of her family. Her father was proud of the fact that all the Francis men had worked with their hands for a living since the first had arrived from England in 1636. An indentured servant he was. His son—Maria's great-grandfather—had become a weaver. And to his son in turn he taught the same craft. Grandfather, she was told, had killed five Redcoats in the fighting at Concord and served four years in Washington's army. Francis men were said to be as sturdy and durable as the cloth they wove.

Maria's father himself—one of ten children—had first been an apprentice baker, then a foreman, and finally, after long years of hard work, had become owner of the bakehouse. His products had a fine reputation, and not only in Medford, which was a Massachusetts town of hardly a thousand people, but everywhere in the country. He was a skillful and inventive man, thorough and scrupulous in what he made and how he sold it. The very tasty and healthful butter cookies he developed and made every step of the way by hand won such wide popularity that people as far off as Russia relished the "Medford crackers."

Now Mr. Francis put down the empty mug and wiped his mouth. He sighed deeply. This July afternoon was so hot and still. Maria watched a lone wasp skitter across the flour-caked table, leaving jagged streaks in its white wake. Suddenly there was the sound of hooves hammering into the ground. What lunatic would be driving so fast on a day like this? They looked up just as the galloping mare tore past the open door of the bakery, dragging the two wheeled carriage behind. A deep, anguished roar split the dusty air. That was Caesar's voice! Mr. Ingraham must be trying to sneak his slave out of town! Mr. Francis sprang for the door, Maria racing behind him. He knew the chaise would be held up by the broken planks in the Medford Bridge that crossed the river running past his door. Clattering onto the bridge, the driver reined in the horse sharply for fear of crippling him. Mr. Francis leaped past the wheels and grabbed the horse's bridle. He motioned to Caesar to jump down and run for it. But the slave, buckled into his seat, was helpless. A pistol flashed in Mr. Ingraham's hand, and Maria's father dropped back. In a few seconds the carriage had rounded the turn and was out of sight.

Mr. Francis stood in the empty road, face scarlet, feet wide apart, arms trembling. Maria had sunk to her knees in the dust, her legs too weak with fear to hold her up. Then her father bent down and scooped her up, holding her tight to his chest. Now she began to cry, quietly, in relief. If he had been run down by the horse, or killed! . . . Stroking her hair gently, Mr. Francis carried her into the shop and set her down.

Now he had to move fast. Quickly he dispatched Convers and the apprentices to rally help. Caesar was a favorite in the village. Years ago, long before Maria was born, the slave had been a tailor in Medford, earning good money for his master. But he had been sold south to a plantation. Many years had passed with no word about him and meantime, as soon as the Revolutionary War had ended, Massachusetts had put a stop to slavery. Then one day, just a few weeks ago, Caesar had suddenly reappeared in Medford, accompanying his master on a business trip.

Maria had seen him in the bakery more than once, telling his old friends what had happened to him. A skilled slave's lot wasn't the worst on the plantation, he had said, but he would give anything to stay in the North. "You don't have to go back, Caesar," Mr. Francis and the others had said. "It's *your* choice now. Slave or no slave, when you're in Massachusetts, you're *free*."

Afraid to tell anyone his plans, Caesar had tried to run away this morning. But Mr. Ingraham, suspicious of the Yankees, had guessed what was up, overtaken Caesar, and now had whirled him out of reach of his friends.

In ten minutes a dozen tradesmen and mechanics had gathered at the bakery. Where would Caesar be hidden? How could they find him? Plans for a search of the surrounding countryside buzzed in the warm, scented air. "No use," said Mr. Francis. "Ingraham's no fool. He must have gone into Boston with Caesar. We'll have trouble. It'll be a long search, and a hard one." "And likely a failure, too," someone else grumbled. They decided to nose about Boston the next day.

But luck was with them. On the coach from Boston to Medford that very evening sat Mr. Ingraham, plump with pride in having outwitted Yankee meddlers. He couldn't keep his satisfaction to himself. He had Caesar safe on shipboard in Boston Harbor, he confided to a neighboring passenger. Behind them sat two ladies—who promptly relayed the information to Caesar's friends.

The next step was simple. A large Medford delegation rode into Boston and obtained the necessary legal papers at the Governor's office. With officers, they proceeded to the ship and brought Caesar off in triumph.

The slaveholder didn't give up a valuable slave that easily. He went into the courts to recover his "property," but clouds of witnesses from Medford appeared each time and Caesar stayed free. That was 1810. Medford took pride in its belief that it was the first town in the United States to rescue a fugitive slave.

Slavery was no new thing in Medford. The village had hardly dug its first houses into the bank of the Mystic River back in 1630 when a Medford sea captain sailed down to the West Indies and sold a cargo of Pequot Indian captives. On his return home he brought a cargo of cotton, tobacco, salt—and Africans. So slavery in Massachusetts had been legal for almost two hundred years. Maria's father had witnessed its end, and rejoiced as the Northern states abolished it one after the other. Often from her bed in the loft of the big brick house Maria could hear the older folks in the kitchen talking into the night, her father getting hot about the shipmasters who were sneaking around the law banning the slave trade, because it meant money in the pockets of the owners and the crews and the merchants who provisioned the swift slavers.

She learned, too, from what she saw about her in the world of work. Besides her father's bakery, there was the blacksmith shop to explore, a tanyard, and the fishing on the Mystic. Bass, shad, and smelts were plentiful. In the spring the great ponds were full of alewives. Dragging a net brought great catches out of the narrow river with its steep banks. The fish were sold chiefly in Boston. But sometimes Maria saw them barrelled and marked for shipment to the Southern states where, she was told, the fish were used for "slave food."

In 1802, the very year Maria was born, neighbor Thomas Magoun laid the first keel of a fleet of merchant ships which she soon watched sailing out to every sea and bay on the navigable globe. A year later, the Middlesex Canal opened, connecting the Merrimack River with Boston Harbor. It was marvelous fun to walk the canal's whole length through Medford, watching the barges and small packets, drawn by two horses, pass through the town's locks.

Shortly before the excitement over Caesar's rescue, another neighbor put the first coach on the road from Medford to Boston. A great enterprise it was, this once-a-day round trip to the capital five miles off. For weeks little

Maria scurried down to the village green to see Mr. Wyman mount his box at 8 A.M., grandly welcoming the ten passengers mustered for the day's journey.

When she was five, Maria attended what was called a "ma'am school." Here she was taught by "Ma'am Betty," a spinster of excessive shyness, who never recovered from the calamity of that day the governor himself caught her drinking water from the nose of her teakettle.

The children met in her bedroom, never a tidy place, and decorated in addition by the tobacco Ma'am Betty always chewed. Later Maria remembered fondly the regular Thanksgiving Eve entertainment to which Ma'am Betty was invited by the Francis family together with the washerwoman, the berrywoman, the wood-sawyer, the journeymen bakers—making twenty or thirty guests in all.

In the big old kitchen they feasted on a giant chicken pie, pumpkin pies made in milk pans, and pyramids of doughnuts. As everyone left the board Maria's mother and father piled crackers and bread and pies high in their arms, adding turnovers for the children.

When Maria's quick mind had taken in all Ma'am Betty had to offer, her father sent her to a seminary. Her progress was rapid, but then, her natural talents were so developed by the companionship of Convers that this finishing school had little to teach her. Convers was a modest and shy boy with an unrelenting hunger for knowledge. He read widely as he prepared for Harvard, and as the years passed he was able to share more of what he learned with Maria. Girls, she found out early, did not have the same chance at education as boys. Convers went off to study for the ministry, leaving a desolate sister behind.

When Maria was twelve, her mother died of tuberculosis. Now she was alone with her father. The other children, all much older, had grown up and gone off. Distraught by his wife's loss, and worried by the unemployment that seized New England as the War of 1812 wore on into still another year, Mr. Francis suddenly sold both his business and his house. But what about Maria? He felt he had so little in common with her. She had grown farther and farther away from him. Indeed, she was different from all the young Medford girls he knew— brighter, more impulsive, heedless of what people would think about anything she did. Without his bakery, he did not know what he would do, nor how Maria would fit into his vague future. So he sent her to live with her newly married sister, Mary, in Maine.

Early separation from home and family seems to have clouded Maria's memories of those years of growing up. When she was a quite a little girl, she recalled years later, she imagined "that gypsies had changed me from some other cradle, and put me in a place where I did not belong."

But she liked Norridgewock. It was a small town along the banks of the Kennebec, and Mary and her young husband, Warren Preston, made her feel at home at once. Maria helped care for the Preston babies as they came along to fill the big clapboard house with shrieks and laughter. She enjoyed making clothes for them and amusing them and the neighborhood children with the stories she invented. At school she studied French and German, and especially history. She didn't want to fall too far behind Convers, at Harvard.

At fifteen, racing through Homer's *Odyssey,* she wrote her brother: "Every passion that he portrayed I felt; I loved, hated, and resented, just as he inspired me!" When she came to *Paradise Lost,* she asked Convers: "Don't you think that Milton asserts superiority of his own sex in rather too lordly a manner?" And when Convers replied that he didn't think so, Maria said her ideas might be wrong, but at least they were her own. She bombarded her brother with questions that came out of her wide reading, often criticizing herself for not thinking carefully and deeply enough. Sir Walter Scott's novels were grand entertainment. "Why cannot I write a novel?" she exclaimed. If she ever did, she thought, she'd try to remember that while gentleness and modesty were fine attributes of girls in real life, in fiction they made for pretty dull going. Then she picked up Gibbon and Shakespeare and Johnson and Addison. She knew more than some of her teachers, and probably took mischievous pleasure in demonstrating it.

In good weather, she would sometimes walk a few

miles up the river to talk with the Abnaki Indians in their bark cabins and buy from them their baskets woven of sweet grass. From them she heard tales of the old days before the white man had come, when they ruled the great pine woods and thought only of hunting and fishing, not of trading baskets. From their melancholy faces and history she absorbed a past that was so recently gone.

Just as she turned eighteen, she sent Convers an excited letter: "I can't talk about books or anything else until I tell you the news!" She was leaving the Preston home to teach school in the town of Gardiner. "I hope, dear brother, that you feel as happy as I do. Not that I have formed any high-flown expectations. All I expect is that, if I am industrious and prudent, I shall be *independent*."

2 ◍ "The Brilliant Miss Francis"

The years Maria taught school in Maine flew by fast. Showered with presents and attention by the townsfolk, she felt a lightness of spirit that charmed the friends she made so easily. She was not a beauty, but her delicate, fresh complexion, her even, white teeth, and her expressive eyes were great assets. She had a determined air of purpose about her, everyone noted, but she was certainly not a starchy Puritan. She loved jokes, and she liked to display her own wit.

One spring day she opened a letter from Convers to find news that made her heart leap. He was to be married in May, he wrote, and he was taking his bride, Abby, to

Watertown, where he had been ordained the new Unitarian minister. And you, Maria, he said, must come live with us. There will be plenty for you to do here, helping Abby with the household duties, and continuing your education in my library.

That was a great turning point for the young girl. She might have managed to achieve great things even if she had spent the rest of her life in Maine villages, but Convers' world would provide infinitely greater nourishment for the talents she still did not know she possessed.

Almost as though she sensed what lay ahead, she asked to be baptized "Maria," and to have that name put down in the parish records. Her parents had named her "Lydia Maria," but from now on it would always be only "Maria."

Convers was "Doctor" Francis now, a title bestowed when he completed his theological studies at the Harvard Divinity School. In the red brick parsonage Maria found herself very much at home. Beyond her window was a lovely rose garden. Watertown was a peaceful old village on the banks of the Charles River, close by Boston. Handsome houses stood back from streets lined with elms and maples.

But to Maria the most exciting aspect of Watertown was Convers' library. This was long before the era of public libraries, and Maria had never seen such riches. Her brother's learning was deep and broad; he seemed to spend every penny on acquiring more and more books.

German literature, French philosophy, American history, biographies, religion, science, encyclopedias, magazines, newspapers—she could go happily blind, Maria felt, in this dazzling world of print.

In his pulpit on Sundays, Convers did not have the power to electrify his hearers. It was at his table and in his study that his intellectual force was felt. His home would become the popular headquarters of the young men and women who called themselves Transcendentalists. Emerson, Thoreau, Theodore Parker, Margaret Fuller, Bronson Alcott—they would explore new paths of thought, battle for the freedom to find their own answers to life's questions.

From Convers Maria learned sound habits of scholarship. She caught his delight in making discoveries about America's early history. This New England soil on which Maria stood was good ground for new thought. The Revolution was only one generation past. Life was not frozen in ancient molds. Prejudices and traditions there were, but not so hardened they could not be moved. No privileged classes had put up walls so high they could not be climbed or torn down.

From the old world came the law, philosophy, science, religion, literature which Convers channeled into Maria's thirsty mind. But he taught her to be discriminating, to examine everything for herself, to accept or dismiss it without regard to its prestige. The Church was no exception, he said. Study its history and traditions while you keep your mind open to fresh currents of criticism.

In her hands, Maria felt, was a life she could shape. At Concord, her grandfather had fired a shot which signaled the birth of individual freedom. Around her brother now, there swirled experiments in thought which tested every truth. Hasn't God chosen this new people to point the way to universal freedom? Having freed ourselves from the old country, can't we work out a society based upon the gospel of humanity? Can't we start with the natural freedom and dignity of man our forefathers proclaimed to the world and make a government and laws that will let man walk upright?

Lofty, brave goals these were. But what could a girl do about them? As Convers and his friends talked of these problems of man's destiny and society's progress Maria must have wondered what her own fate would be. She was of the smaller and weaker sex (though, as she said, that didn't seem to bother men when they hired laundresses and scrubwomen). In book after book she had found the assertion that just as woman's physical powers were inferior to man's, so were her mental powers. Frail. Meek. Gentle. Submissive. Humble . . . . Were these the only virtues for a woman? No, there was modesty, too. That was her crowning virtue, a virtue she was supposed to be born with. It meant not only a delicacy in speech and manner but a withdrawal from the rough-and-tumble world of men and issues, from the competition of the marketplace.

One Sunday in the summer of 1824, Maria was thumbing through an old issue of a magazine in her brother's study when she stopped at a review of a poem with the odd title "Yamoyden." It was a tale of the Indian wars led by King Philip. We are glad somebody has at last seen that our own history can be woven into poetry, the reviewer said. Why don't more of our American writers make as effective use of the early days of New England as Sir Walter Scott did of his native history?

It was noon when Maria came across that passage. Years earlier, reading Scott for the first time in Maine, she had wondered if she could write a novel. This challenge must have stirred that old impulse into action. A couple of hours later, when Convers came in to take her to his afternoon service, she looked up from a desk covered with sheets of scrawled paper. She had written the first chapter of a novel. With Convers' encouragement, she completed the story within a few months. Before the year was up the novel was published by a Boston firm.

Hobomok: A Tale of Early Times, it was titled. She signed it "By an American." Almost overnight, the novel became a success. Everyone was talking about it and asking who the author was.

Hobomok was named after one of its major characters, a young Indian who lived with his tribe on the edge of the new settlement of Salem. He has been hopelessly in love with Mary Conant, the daughter of an English settler, but she loves another man, Charles Brown. When she hears that Brown has been lost at sea, she turns in desolation to Hobomok, who elopes with her against her father's wishes.

Later, after Hobomok and Mary have had a child, Brown reappears in Salem, and Hobomok, understanding that Mary still loves the other man, disappears into the forest.

Maria's story caught public interest for several reasons. She was one of the first American writers to turn to the Indians for material. By her time the Indians were no longer felt to be a menace in New England, and there was a great curiosity about the red man, about his way of life and his history.

Although Maria's portrait of Hobomok was conventional and romantic—he seems impossibly noble now— she was very daring in presenting an interracial marriage. While readers rushed to get her book, one critic attacked her for permitting a virtuous Puritan maiden to marry an Indian and to bear his child. "It is in very bad taste, to say the least, and leaves upon the mind a disagreeable impression," commented the *North American Review.*

But most readers evidently relished the novelty of a very independent heroine who dares to defy her bigoted father. The father, pious as he is, shows up poorly in contrast with the primitive Hobomok, who gives up his own happiness for the sake of others.

It took very little time for it to get about that this provocative novel had been written by Lydia Maria Francis, a woman, a young woman, and a single one at that! The very proper people were appalled. This "female exhibition in publick" broke all the rules for correct behavior. Anticipating this, Maria had tried to conceal her authorship. Let the book speak for itself, she thought. She recalled that when she was a child in Medford, the aged Hannah Adams was pointed out as a great curiosity because she had written a history of New England. Why, said the indignant gossips, she has become so learned she has lost her femininity! She never knows when she has a hole in her stocking and she is absolutely unable to recognize her own face in the mirror—and if *that* isn't being unfeminine, pray tell us what could be!

When *Hobomok's* authorship was discovered, some women hastened to tell Maria that having written a book she could no longer expect to be regarded as a *lady*. The news did not crush her. How could she help but enjoy all the attention she was getting? Within another year she was ready with her second novel, *The Rebels; or, Boston before the Revolution*. Still, she did not sign her name to it. This time, the title page read: "By the author of *Hobomok.*"

Her choice of the subject may have been prompted by

the fact that 1825 was the fiftieth anniversary of the first battles of the Revolution. At hand in Convers' library were the historical documents she needed and on the streets of Boston she could talk to many survivors of those heroic times whose living memory could enrich her story.

In her second novel Maria again made her heroine, Lucretia, a woman who stood by her beliefs, a woman who refused to marry the man of her guardian's choice. Lucretia (she might well have been called "Maria") knew what she wanted out of life and did not intend to waste it.

Maria, only twenty-three and as yet with little real experience of the world, showed herself quite adept at mixing historical figures with imaginary characters. Her plot was too complicated and tricky, but her people were real, so real that an imaginary sermon she put in the mouth of the preacher George Whitefield and an imaginary speech she had the orator James Otis make were taken as authentic and declaimed for generations out of school readers.

The Rebels was "most respectfully inscribed" to George Ticknor. Mr. Ticknor, a Harvard professor of modern languages, born in the upper crust of Boston society, had discovered the richness of popular legends as a source for literature. When *Hobomok* appeared, he welcomed Maria into his fashionable drawing room on Beacon Hill. There she sat down to his famous suppers with Boston's notables and the pick of visiting strangers at her elbow. Discussing diplomacy, travel, literature, science in this intimate circle, young Maria soon became "the brilliant Miss Francis." Her wit and vivacity made her the delight of evenings that often included the great Daniel Webster, the preacher Dr. William Ellery Channing, the Prescotts, the Everetts, the Bowditches. It was the beginning of a new age for Boston, an age in which for a generation at least she was to dominate the country's intellectual life.

Maria's prestige as one of the leading young authors brought her an invitation from the Governor to attend his reception for General Lafayette, who was visiting Boston to take part in the fiftieth anniversary celebration of the Battle of Bunker Hill. There her hand was kissed by the French hero, and later she may have met him again at Mr. Ticknor's supper party.

Such continued success, in literature and in society, must have been deliciously exciting to young Maria. Yet that very year she opened a private school in Watertown. The baker's daughter had been brought up in the conviction that it took hard work to make a living. Perhaps she couldn't believe that writing novels would earn her way. Thus far in young America hardly any men had been able to live by their pen. As for ambitions in society, she said "it has often been hinted to me that I should stand a great deal better with the upper classes if I would avoid mentioning that my father was a mechanic." That she would not do. She made nothing of the accident of birth.

"I am not proud of my father's being a mechanic," she said, "but neither am I ashamed of it."

As a distinguished author, and the sister of the town minister, she had no trouble finding pupils. And regularly publishers knocked at her door to see what new success she might have ready for them.

3 &c Maria Marries

It was a fascinating guest Convers had invited home this evening. The usually talkative Maria sat silent and wide-eyed, listening to stories of adventures abroad that might have been torn out of Scott's novels. The stranger opposite Maria was thirty-year-old David Lee Child. He was describing the life he had seen in many countries of Europe during the four years of his diplomatic service. He had been in the legation at Madrid last year when the king invited a French army in to help him put down a rising revolution. David watched Madrid occupied by the foreign troops, the people's hatred swelling against the tyranny, bombs exploding in the streets. Unable to stand by, he had resigned his post and seized a rifle to join in the hopeless battle to oust the invaders.

For hours now he talked, sketching the contrasts in life abroad—the painfully slow improvements in Italy, the ancient farming methods of Spain where the plow Vergil described was still in use, and against these the hurry and bustle of England's mad scramble into the new age of industrialism.

Of old Puritan stock, Mr. Child was a Harvard graduate who had taught school for a few years before getting his appointment in Europe. Now he was in Watertown to study law with his uncle. In this small place there were plenty of chances for him to meet the young novelist he had heard so much about. After the next encounter, at Mrs. Curtis', Maria confided to her journal: "He is the most gallant man that has lived since the 16th century, and needs nothing but helmet, shield, and chain-armor to make him a complete knight of chivalry." A few months later (it was the spring of 1825): "I do not know which to admire most, the vigor of his understanding, or the ready sparkle of his wit."

They saw each other now and then, but spoke nothing of their inmost feelings. Then, when David was asked to come to Boston to edit a political weekly, he was astonished to find he was made more miserable than happy by the offer. If he accepted, it would plunge him into the political battles he loved. But it also meant he would see much less of Maria. He had little choice, however, for he was still preparing for the bar and he needed to earn a living.

Maria, meanwhile, was shaping a new idea in her mind, an idea that came out of her experience teaching school. Children must learn to read, but they should enjoy the learning. Yet there was so little literature written especially for them. Then why not start a children's magazine?

She took her idea to Boston and returned with a contract from a publisher to edit a ninety-page magazine that would come out every two months. In September, 1826, the first issue of the *Juvenile Miscellany* appeared. It was the pioneer children's magazine in America and an immediate success. Young readers found it a cheerful and entertaining companion.

Its style was simple and natural. As Maria said years later when many more books and magazines for children had begun to appear, she detested baby-talk literature. She never wrote down to her readers or forced morals down their throats.

She saw to it that her illustrators worked in the same way. I can't stand drawings that show children as dolls or as grown folks cut shorter, she told her artists. As the magazine gained popularity with each issue, children sent gifts or brought flowers to "the lady who told such good stories in the *Miscellany*."

In Boston, David's editorship pushed him into the political spotlight and his warm, energetic personality helped win him a seat in the state legislature. He wasn't getting very far with his law practice, but then, he found it hard to become interested in commercial cases. He thought it time, anyhow, to propose to Maria. It took him four hours to win her yes, but in the end he got it. The news upset Maria's family. David clearly was not practicing law for the fees he could get out of it. Maria was foolish to marry a dreamer, they thought. But to her, David's idealism was not a fault.

In October, 1828, they were married. They set up housekeeping in a manner that was to be typical of them all their long life together. For the first few years they lived in a little box of a house on Harvard Street near David's office in the center of Boston. Then, when David became a justice of the peace, they found a small home outside the city, where she could fill a tiny garden with flowers. The sea dashed under their windows and was often sparkling with moonbeams when they went to bed.

They lived very simply with plain furniture bought largely out of Maria's literary earnings. She hired no domestic help, doing all her own cleaning and washing and cooking, a practice that caused comment from some of her more elegant friends. Maria was an excellent cook, and she liked to entertain, but she planned her chores so as to spend the minimum amount of time at them. She wanted to hold on to the best hours of each day for her writing.

She had hardly settled into domestic life when one

night David challenged her with a question he had been taking up in his newspaper. What could she do to help save the Cherokee Indians from "that monster," General Jackson? Uprooted a generation ago from their hunting grounds in Georgia, the Cherokees had moved across the mountains into the northwest corner of the state. Recently gold had been discovered on their land, and whites had rushed in, shoving the Indians back. Federal troops ordered in by President John Quincy Adams had protected the Cherokees. But now the new president, Andrew Jackson, had changed government policy. Nothing any longer stood between the Indians and the greedy gold-diggers.

Through his newspaper, David was trying to rally all lovers of liberty to the Cherokee cause. But what could Maria do? She had always felt sympathy for the Indians in the injustices they suffered. In *Hobomok* she had shown that. Now she saw a new way to help—by reaching adults and children at the same time with an appeal for the Indians. She would put what she had to say in the form of a dialogue between a mother and her two daughters.

She got to work at once, drawing on the early histories of the Pequot and Narraganset Indians of New England. Her book was called *The First Settlers of New England*. "I ardently hope," she told her readers, "that this unvarnished tale will impress our youth with the conviction of their obligation to alleviate, as much as is in their power, the sufferings of the generous and interesting race of men we have so unjustly supplanted."

She tried to make clear that racial prejudice was at the root of the merciless way whites were driving Indians off their own homeland. It was a prejudice that went back to the religious bigotry of old Puritans, she said. Many of the first settlers thought God had ordained them to conquer the "red devils." They were chosen to do God's work, were they not? Hence any action they took was in His name. An easy excuse, this, to rob, beat, exile, and even kill the Indians.

David and Maria did their best, but editorials and pamphlets alone were poor weapons against greed and race hatred. The tribesmen took their case to the Supreme Court. It ruled in their favor, but President Jackson refused to enforce the decision. Bribery, fraud, and force drove fifteen thousand Cherokees into exile and death.

The first year of marriage went by, with Maria learning many of the little economies of good housewifery. To make ends meet, she had to be creative. As soon as things were running smoothly, she thought of a way to convert all those cheese parings and candle ends into cash. Why not write a book about domestic economy? Think of all the housewives who shared her problems! Attacked with her usual directness, the book was soon done. She called it *The Frugal Housewife*. In its first year, it sold six thousand copies. By 1834, five years after publication, fourteen editions had been printed. For years it was one of the most popular and valued books in American households. Abroad, it went through twelve editions in England and Scotland, and nine in Germany.

A cookbook—and something more—it was dedicated "To Those Who Are Not Ashamed of Economy." Maria claimed that if it followed her advice, a family could live comfortably on $600 a year. Nothing expensive was in her recipes; all were healthful and useful (although one of Maria's cakes required three pounds of butter and twenty-eight eggs).

She listed what cuts of meat to buy and advised buying them in quantity, told how to corn or dry-cure, urged baking one's own bread and cake. There were recipes for beer and wine, too. Beer, combined with New England rum, helped make very good pancakes. And it seems the rum was also good for shampoo, the whiskey for ringworm, and the gin for cement.

Sprinkled among the recipes were little essays on economy, enlivened by anecdotes of wives who lost their husbands' affection because they teased too much for money. Extravagance, she warned, was the nation's vice, and even New England was giving in to it. Young ladies of the day were showing vanity, extravagance, and idleness because they were taught only elegancies and ornaments at school. If they were to grow into something better than "man-traps," they must learn more useful things, Maria said.

So eager did readers seem for Maria's advice that she

quickly put two more manuals on the market. In *The Mother's Book* she pointed out that it was no longer enough to train girls to be wives and mothers. They needed to know something about the business side of household affairs. No doubt this advice came straight from the heart, for it was already painfully clear to Maria that David would never manage well.

The Girl's Own Book must have been as much a delight to young readers as it was a relief to mothers desperate for ideas to distract a houseful of children. It was chockful of things to do: games (150 of them); charades; enigmas; puzzles; conundrums; instructions for knitting, crocheting, tatting and needlework; maxims for health and gracefulness; how to dance, skip rope, swing, shoot with bow and arrow, make baskets, garden, keep bees, and write poetry.

These books, too, ran into many editions. No young writer was better known in all New England, in all these United States. Lydia Maria Child could write about anything, it seemed, and people would want to read it.

From the *North American Review,* the most important of all literary journals, came these words of praise:

We are not sure that any woman of our country could outrank Mrs. Child. This lady has long been before the public with much success. And well she deserves it, for in all her works nothing can be found

which does not commend itself .... Few female
writers if any have done more or better things for our
literature in the lighter or graver departments.

She could have gone on as a popular, noncontroversial
lady writer, earning more and more money, making life
easier and more comfortable for herself and David, if it
had not been for a young man who set out to change
America's way of thinking.

4 ☍ An Appeal

Fourth of July orators still liked to remind their listeners of the tyranny of England. After all, it was hardly fifty years since American arms had won independence from British power. Satisfied smiles would spread over Boston faces at those ringing words, "O sons of freedom!"

But this time, in 1829, there was a different text. Park Street Church was experimenting with a newcomer, young William Lloyd Garrison. He was a nobody, really, this twenty-three-year-old printer who had pestered the ministers until they had granted him the privilege of making the Fourth of July address.

Now his tall, lean, black-coated figure was in the

pulpit. His legs trembled and his voice quavered as he began. The large audience strained forward to hear the first feeble sentences. Then, as he gathered confidence, his voice took on deeper tones.

"I stand up here to obtain the liberation of two millions of wretched, degraded beings, who are pining in hopeless bondage—over whose sufferings scarcely an eye weeps, or a heart melts, or a tongue pleads either to God or man."

He flung his challenge to the frock-coated Bostonians. Our politics are rotten to the core. Slavery is a national sin, and we are all alike guilty. New England money has bought human flesh, New England ships have carried black cargoes, New England men have helped forge the fetters of those who groan in bondage. It is the duty of men in the free states, who were constitutionally involved in the guilt of slavery, to speak out against its continuance, and to assist in its overthrow.

Why delay the work? There must be a beginning! *Now* is the time!

It was an effective speech, packed with facts into a powerful argument. This stranger was reaching some hearts that were sick, sick of the lie they knew their country was living. The sin of slavery might not be on their tongues, but it was in everyone's mind. Here was a new nation, which held it a self-evident truth that all men are created equal, endowed by their Creator with the unalienable rights of life, liberty, and the pursuit of happiness—and here too was the horrible fact of human slavery.

Once the issue had been discussed, at the Constitutional Convention. But the Southern delegates had threatened to withdraw if slavery were questioned. And ever since a policy of silence had ruled.

But the issue of slavery did not go away. Jefferson, an old man at Monticello, could not bury it. "This momentous question, like a fire-bell in the night, awakened and filled me with terror."

And now here was William Lloyd Garrison, determined not to let Boston's leaders hush the bell. To some who heard Garrison that day, it was the lifting of a great stone from their hearts. They had forgotten the sound of truth. When he stepped down from the pulpit, all Boston knew who he was.

To David Child, Garrison was no stranger. They had met when Garrison found work setting type for David's paper. A few months after his Fourth of July speech, Garrison went to Baltimore to help Benjamin Lundy edit his antislavery journal.

David, too, was catching sparks from abolition's bonfire. In the state legislature he had already denounced the slaveholders' threats to annex Mexico, and then had published a powerful pamphlet against it. Maria did not always agree with him. The Boston papers were loudly accusing the antislavery men of sedition and fanaticism. Charges that the abolitionists wanted to send fire and sword into the South, and encourage the slaves to hunt down their masters, troubled her. She was against slavery

—from her childhood in Medford—but was the call for immediate and unconditional emancipation the right way to go about it? If slavery was wrong, why put off freedom for one minute? David replied. They argued about it night after night. Her prejudice against the movement was strong, he saw. It was hard to overcome the effect of a steady bombardment of newspaper editorials. But once he had made her stop taking charges for granted, without pausing to investigate, she began to see her mistakes.

Then news came that Garrison had been thrown into a Baltimore jail for calling a New England shipowner a "highway robber and murderer" because he carried slave cargoes. For seven weeks Garrison sat in prison, writing private letters and public letters, pamphlets and poems, receiving visitors, and winning new converts to his cause.

Released from jail, he came to Boston seeking support for a new journal to be devoted to abolition.

Maria had a talk with him. "It is wonderful how one mortal may affect the destiny of a multitude," she said later. "I remember very distinctly the first time I ever saw Garrison. I little thought then that the whole pattern of my life-web would be changed by that introduction . . . . He got hold of the strings of my conscience and pulled me into reforms. It is of no use to imagine what might have been, if I had never met him. Old dreams vanished, old associates departed, and all things became new."

It was at about this time that Maria received a note from the trustees of the Boston Athenaeum, offering her the complimentary use of their fine private library. It was a signal honor—only one other woman, Hannah Adams, had ever been granted that privilege. Maria had not asked the favor; she guessed that Professor Ticknor had probably suggested it.

The best use she could make of it, she decided, would be to study slavery. For she had decided to write a book about it . . . .

As Maria began tracing slavery's roots in the old documents in the Athenaeum's quiet rooms, outside the sound of thunder was beginning to be heard. On New Year's Day, 1831, the first issue of Garrison's small four-page paper, the *Liberator,* appeared. Swiftly word spread among the Negro freemen of the new fighter for Negro rights. Subscriptions came in from Boston, Philadelphia, New York. David Child and a few other whites climbed the stairs to the shabby little editorial offices to offer their encouragement. The gentle minister Samuel J. May suggested perhaps Garrison's editorials were too harsh, too undiplomatic? The substantial citizens of Boston would take offense. That was exactly his intention, Garrison replied. He would damn and torment the complacent until their consciences awoke. For anyone—businessman, preacher, professor—to be silent in the face of slavery was to share in the guilt of its existence.

That summer, terror blazed in a Virginia slave revolt that left fifty-seven whites dead. The uprising, led by the Negro preacher Nat Turner, was blamed by Southerners upon that "incendiary" newspaper, the *Liberator*. Yet Garrison had not a single subscriber south of the Potomac. A hundred Southern editors, exchanging their papers with his, frightened themselves and their readers by quoting from the *Liberator*.

Yes, Garrison's voice was being heard. But he himself knew his influence was exaggerated. He had only fifty white subscribers, half of them in Boston, and mostly friends. Three fourths of his readers were Negroes. If their abolitionism was to get anywhere, it needed a real organization. So as 1831 neared its end, several men met in lawyer Samuel Sewall's office to talk over Garrison's plan. One of the men was David Child. Out of their discussion came the New England Anti-slavery Society, with the *Liberator* its official voice, and David Child and Ellis Gray Loring its counselors. The society pledged itself to immediate freedom for the slave, by peaceful and lawful means; to improvement of the free Negro's condition; and to opposition to attempts to ship free Negroes to Africa.

One of the *Liberator's* readers took fire from Garrison's message and tried to do something herself about improving the Negro's condition. She was Miss Prudence Crandall. In 1833 she opened a boarding school for Negro girls in Canterbury, Connecticut. The state legislature promptly put a law through making it a crime to teach colored girls in Connecticut.

The Negro girls were insulted and stoned on the streets, the school wrecked and burned, and finally Miss Crandall was forced to give up. Many Northerners had been telling the abolitionists to go South, where the slaves were, to do their agitating. The Crandall case showed how much there was to be done right here at home. The long arm of the slaveholders had reached into the North. Free colored people were not citizens, the Canterbury lawyer claimed in court; the state therefore had a perfect right to pass laws discriminating against their children.

"They seem to assume," Maria wrote, "that the colored people *must* always be an inferior and degraded class— that the prejudice against *them* must be eternal, as though founded in the laws of God and nature!"

Violent opposition to education of the Negro erupted almost everywhere. Seeing prejudice and hostility displayed again and again in the free states, David and some of his abolitionist friends became trustees of a new interracial school in New Hampshire. Noyes Academy, they said, would "afford colored youth a fair opportunity to show that they are capable, equally with the whites, of improving themselves in every scientific attainment, every social virtue, and every Christian ornament."

The school attracted interest in many states. It opened in the village of Canaan with twenty-eight whites and fourteen Negroes attending classes. But as soon as studies began, prejudice got to work. "Fourteen black boys with books in their hands," wrote one of them, "set the entire Granite State crazy!"

Newspaper attacks built up to a town meeting which advocated abolishing the school "in the interest of the town, the honor of the state, and the good of the whole community." A great mob paraded to the academy and, with a team of one hundred yoke of oxen, dragged the school building from its foundations and left it a useless wreck. The job done, the mob leaders met to condemn abolitionism for trying to destroy the liberty the Revolutionary Fathers had died for.

What harm could Negro education possibly do us? Maria asked. Yet everywhere it came up for discussion, she observed, "the demon of prejudice girds himself for the battle."

She decided to make an attack upon race prejudice a central part of her book, and speeded up her writing. Late in 1833 there came off the press *An Appeal in Favor of That Class of Americans Called Africans*. She dedicated it to the Reverend Samuel J. May, in gratitude for his defense of Prudence Crandall.

Maria knew her problem in finding readers for a book on so unpopular a cause. In her preface, she tried to disarm opposition:

"Reader, I beseech you not to throw down this volume as soon as you have glanced at the title. Read it, if your prejudices will allow, for the very truth's sake: Read it, from sheer curiosity to see what a woman (who had much better attend to her household concerns) will say upon such a subject . . . .

"Should it be the means of advancing, even one single hour, the inevitable progress of truth and justice, I would not exchange the consciousness for all Rothschild's wealth, or Sir Walter's fame."

Maria's book—it was the first antislavery volume to be published in the United States—was equally distinguished as one of the early arguments against racial prejudice. "We first debase the nature of man by making him a slave," she pointed out, "and then very coolly tell him that he must always remain a slave because he does not know how to use freedom. We first crush people to the earth, and then claim the right of trampling on them forever, because they are prostrate. Truly, human selfishness never invented a rule which worked out so charmingly both ways!"

To the common charge that Negroes were after all fit to be slaves, for when did they ever resist it? she replied:

"By thousands and thousands, these poor people have died for freedom. They have stabbed themselves for freedom—jumped into the waves for freedom—starved for freedom—fought like very tigers for freedom! But they have been hung, and burned, and shot—and their tyrants have been their historians!"

Of course there are now many ignorant and illiterate Negroes, she said. "But this ceases to be the case just in proportion as they are free. The fault is in their unnatural situation, not in themselves." Children treated with violence and contempt and denied the chance to learn are called fools by the very people who have crushed their mental energies.

She fired a broadside at "the common and most absurd apology for personal prejudice—the intellectual inferiority of the Negro." Early as it was in the development of the sciences of anthropology and biology, she knew the facts well enough to show that all races are alike in the range of mental abilities. Each has the same potential for growth and development and high achievement.

To prove this is true of the Negro, she drew on history for the accomplishments of many African nations—in the arts, the sciences, mechanics, agriculture, government. And she illustrated her point with thumbnail sketches of Negroes who had distinguished themselves in various fields.

While I attack slavery, she said, I don't mean to flatter myself that we in the North are any better. "The *form* of slavery doesn't exist among us, but the very *spirit* of the hateful thing is here in all its strength."

Our prejudice against the Negro, she maintained, is just as deep-seated and chronic. In what schools are Negroes treated equally? In what theater can they get a decent seat? In what church do they share our pews? In what restaurant do we dine together? In what boat or stagecoach or railroad or streetcar are they not segregated? To what business—besides cutting hair, shining shoes, or waiting on table—are they allowed to aspire? What Negro on our streets does not have boys dogging his footsteps with the cry of "Nigger! Nigger!"

Yet, Maria went on, who in this country dared, until very recently, to publish anything on this subject? "Our books, our reviews, our newspapers, our almanacs, have all been silent, or exerted their influence on the wrong side. The Negro's crimes are repeated, but his sufferings are never told."

We made slavery, she said, and slavery makes the prejudice. "Let us no longer act upon the narrow-minded idea that we must always continue to do wrong, because we have so long been in the habit of doing it."

What can be done about it? Much, very much, she said. And she cited what the Quakers were doing for conscience' sake, and what the Anti-slavery Society stood for. Their object was to turn the public against this evil, by plain talk about the facts.

Maria warned her readers that ridicule and reproach would be heaped upon any who joined the antislavery cause. "Power, wealth, talent, pride" are all in arms against us, she said.

But "the gold was never coined for which I would barter my individual freedom of acting and thinking upon any subject, or knowingly interfere with the rights of the meanest human being. The only true courage is that which impels us to do right without regard of consequences."

Maria had need of that kind of courage, for the consequences to her of publishing the *Appeal* were terrible, and swift.

"I felt as though I had marched into the enemy's camp, alone," she said. Only yesterday the leading literary magazines had all hailed her. She was the most popular woman writer in the country, South as well as North. And suddenly, for lending her pen to the cause of the slave, an overwhelming tide of abuse swept over her.

The respectables of Beacon Hill, the elegant men and women of George Ticknor's circle, who had patronized Maria for almost ten years, at once shut their doors against her. The sales of her other books dropped disastrously. Outraged mothers canceled subscriptions for the *Juvenile Miscellany,* and within a year the magazine was dead.

Of course she sent the Boston Athenaeum a copy of her *Appeal.* A few weeks later, a trustee let her know she was no longer welcome. They had not expected the privilege they extended her would be used for this horrid subject. A prominent lawyer picked up the *Appeal* with tongs and flung the obnoxious book out of his window.

It was "a sad record," commented Wendell Phillips, the great abolitionist, years later. But "the young author never faltered. Hardly ever was there a costlier sacrifice. Narrow means just changing to ease; after a weary struggle, fame and social position in her grasp; every door opening before her; the sweetness of having her genius recognized . . .

"No one had supposed that independence of opinion on a moral question would wreck all this. It was a thunderbolt from a summer sky. But confronted suddenly with the alternative—gagged life or total wreck—she never hesitated."

The *Appeal* was sneered at and denounced in high places, but it brought great joy to the abolitionists. Very widely read, it won converts to the cause of antislavery. It appealed to reason and to the heart. Its calm, strong tone, its systematic treatment, its careful statements, made it the most convincing book for the times.

Maria sent a copy to William Ellery Channing, New England's great Unitarian leader. In a few days he came out to see her, walking all the way from Mt. Vernon street to Cottage Place. For three hours they sat and talked. It was a strange meeting. Many of the abolitionists were bitter about Channing, who had kept silent on slavery lest he lose the support of parishioners and public. But now, he told Maria, her book had stirred up his mind to the conviction that he ought not to remain silent on the issue.

Again and again Channing sent for her, relying on her for reports of developments in the antislavery struggle. She felt, she said, "like a busy mouse, gnawing away the network which aristocratic family and friends are all the time weaving around the lion." When Channing issued his own pamphlet, *Slavery,* the exposé found its way into many parlors which would never have accepted the *Liberator.* And so from mind to mind and from heart to heart the flame leaped.

Another ally brought to Maria's door by her *Appeal* was Dr. John Gorham Palfrey, distinguished Harvard professor and historian. Years afterward, when he emancipated slaves he had inherited in the South, he traced his action to the impulse her book had given him.

In Connecticut, where Samuel J. May had been struggling to defend Prudence Crandall, the book with its dedication to him came as a complete surprise. Deeply moved, he said, "Now, indeed, I *must* go forward; I can never draw back."

That winter Wendell Phillips, the handsome and brilliant young Bostonian, son of a leading family, confided to friends that he had been reading the *Appeal* "and didn't know but he should be obliged to come out an abolitionist!" Very soon he was to take his place in antislavery leadership side by side with Garrison.

In liberating herself from the petty anxieties which were the common lot of women, Maria helped many a man to find his way out of a life of quiet desperation.

5 ☙❧ The Mob Year

Soon after Maria's *Appeal,* pamphlets, newspapers, magazines, and books poured from the antislavery presses. Maria's pen was never still. As though roused by the respectable opposition to her *Appeal,* she followed it up at once with *The Oasis,* a collection of antislavery pieces. Then within two years came *An Antislavery Catechism, The Evils of Slavery and the Cure of Slavery,* and *Authentic Narratives of American Slavery.*

These joined the many other weapons in the abolition-ist arsenal. Not physical force, but moral persuasion, was their method. They fought their battle with reason, but reason swung like an ax against irrationality; with conscience, but conscience thrust like a bayonet into wrong-doing.

Paper was plentiful in those times, but people were few. If you counted abolitionist noses you wondered how so tiny a band dared oppose government, business, law, society. They stood naked and alone in those early years, defenseless against the vast majority. Yet they had an idea, a cause, and by the moral power and passion of a few individuals they soon began to touch the conscience of the nation.

They thought of slavery as a national sin. They were martyrs willing to suffer persecution to win converts to the truth of their cause. (Had not Jesus said that no greater love has man than to lay down his life for his friends?)

Again and again they would be given the chance to test their courage. For Maria one of the earliest trials came soon after she joined the Boston Female Anti-slavery Society. Lucretia Mott had been the first American woman to make history when, although only a spectator, she dared to speak up at the convention which formed the American Antislavery Society. Others swiftly followed her example and soon there were women's auxiliaries to many local antislavery societies.

It was hard enough to face the traditional prejudices against women, but abolitionist women had to endure much worse. The antislavery speeches and pamphlets and newspapers were reaching out everywhere. Quoted in the

Southern press, they roused the slaveholders to fury. Cries of "fanatic," "traitor," "jacobin," "cut-throat," "infidel," were hurled against Garrison and all his followers.

"These dangerous men agitate a question that must not be tampered with," said one Boston paper. "They are plotting the destruction of our government, and they must not be allowed to screen themselves from the enormity of their guilt."

A letter from James Hammond of South Carolina appeared in one New York paper insisting that abolitionists be "silenced in but one way—*Terror—Death.*"

By 1835 the air was heavy with anger. In the abolitionist newspapers appeared report after report of agents mobbed everywhere. In one week an editor counted over one hundred press reports of mob violence.

When meetings were broken up by force, the press congratulated the mobs instead of condemning them. They blamed not those who swung clubs and threw stones but those who insisted on their right to hold meetings to discuss slavery. The screws tightened as banks and insurance companies, merchants and manufacturers, bishops and editors sought to turn the abolitionists from their goals.

Disgusted by the mobs, and fearful for Maria's safety, her brother Convers wrote her that democracy seemed to be the mother of evil. No, she replied, the aristocracy, "unable to act openly, disguises itself and sends its poison from under a mask. What is the root of the difficulty on this great question of abolition? It is not with the farmers, it is not with the mechanics . . . No, no! It is not those who are to blame for the persecution suffered by abolitionists. Manufacturers who supply the South, merchants who trade with the South, politicians who trade with the South, ministers settled at the South, and editors patronized by the South, are the ones who really promote mobs."

Proof that Maria was right came one day when Rev. Samuel J. May was called from the platform of an abolitionist meeting in New York. A prominent merchant collared him at the door and said:

"Mr. May, we are not such fools as not to know that slavery is a great evil, a great wrong. But it was consented to by the founders of our Republic. It was provided for by the Constitution of our union. A great portion of the property of the Southerners is invested under its sanction; and the business of the North as well as the South has become adjusted to it. There are millions upon millions of dollars due from Southerners to the merchants and mechanics of New York alone, the payment of which would be jeopardized by any rupture between the North and the South. We cannot afford, sir, to let you and your associates succeed in your endeavor to overthrow slavery. It is not a matter of principle with us, it is a matter of business necessity. We cannot afford to let you succeed; and I have called you out to let you know, and to let your fellow-laborers know, that we do not mean to allow you to succeed. We mean, sir, to put you Abolitionists down— by fair means if we can, by foul means if we must."

Such Northerners sat in the best pews in the churches and were trustees of the best colleges. They owned the newspapers and they directed the publishing houses. And often they owned the men who sat in the legislatures. With their active support or silent consent the reign of terror which made 1835 "the mob year" mounted higher and higher.

That July, a ferocious anti-Negro riot broke out in Philadelphia when a colored servant struck his employer. News flashed north of a slave insurrection plot in Mississippi, with two white abolitionists lynched for promoting it. On the night of July 29, the leading citizens of Charleston, South Carolina, broke into the post office and grabbed a pile of abolitionist literature just arrived by mail packet from New York and, in Southern eyes, intended to incite slave insurrection. The next night three thousand people gathered around a huge bonfire to watch Charleston "purify by fire" the abolition pamphlets and to hang Garrison in effigy.

In these circumstances, said Postmaster General Amos Kendall in Washington, he could not condemn the destruction of mail nor the violation of freedom of the press.

Southern newspapers demanded that the North show its sympathy "by *works* as well as by words." Maria felt the hurricane excitement. George Thompson, the young British abolitionist orator, was on a speaking tour of the East, lending his aid to the Americans. Rage against this "roving foreign incendiary" mounted higher and higher.

Early in August Thompson was attacked at two meetings in Lynn, Massachusetts, on one occasion escaping from the hands of three hundred rioters only when the ladies escorted him out. David and Maria accompanied him to New York and hid him for a while in the homes of friends. From New York, Maria wrote, the excitement was so great it could not be imagined. "'Tis like the times of the French Revolution, when no man dared trust his neighbors . . . . Very large sums are offered for anyone who will convey Mr. Thompson into the Slave States. I tremble for him . . . in the terrible state of fermentation now existing here."

A few months earlier, Thompson had spoken at a meeting Maria had attended in Boston. The owner of the Tremont House had brought to the hall a large number of his slaveholding guests, who were staying in town to make their annual purchases of the merchants.

Spotting them in the audience the eloquent Thompson felt inspired. He poured denunciation on their heads till they could not hold back their anger. Finally, one of them shouted, "If we had you down South, we'd cut off your ears!" Folding his arms, Thompson looked calmly at the man, and replied, "Well, sir, if you did cut off my ears, I should still cry aloud, 'he that *hath* ears to hear, let him hear.'"

Maria's heart was thumping violently, for just as the meeting had begun, the abolitionists had noticed a large group of powerful truckmen gathered by the door, hired by the Southerners to seize Thompson and carry him off to a South Carolina ship waiting at the Long Wharf. Maria and a group of the antislavery women had agreed on a plan to forestall the kidnapping. As soon as Thompson finished, she and the others ran up on the platform and, gathering round him, appeared to be discussing the meeting. But as they talked, they kept moving back toward a rear curtain. When they reached it, they were closed tight around the Englishman, and he was able to disappear behind it without anyone in the audience noticing. He jumped out a back door, and leaped into a carriage with swift horses, kept waiting for him. The Southerners were standing tiptoe to survey the platform and suddenly noticed their quarry was missing. "He's gone!" they bellowed, and they thundered down the front stairs to catch him in the street. But it was too late; Thompson was minutes out of sight. They could not figure out how he had escaped, for none but a few of the abolitionists knew of the door behind the curtain.

Thompson kept on, but when he and the poet Whittier were almost lynched in New Hampshire, his American friends induced him again to stop lecturing till the country's fever would subside. He moved from hiding place to hiding place, aided by Maria and David. In October it was announced he would speak again, in Boston, but the hall's owner withdrew his permission. Meanwhile a false rumor spread that he would appear at the meeting of the

Boston Female Anti-slavery Society on October 21. A broadside appeared on the streets calling on "the friends of the Union" to "snake out the infamous foreign scoundrel Thompson" and bring him to the tar kettle.

When about twenty of the women met that afternoon in their room next door to the *Liberator* office, a mob of a thousand men, "led by many gentlemen of property and influence," gathered on the street below. They broke into the meeting, hunting for Mr. Thompson. Mayor Lyman arrived and asked the women to leave. "Indeed, ladies, you must retire," he said. "It is dangerous to remain." But Maria Weston Chapman replied, "If this is the last bulwark of freedom, we may as well die here as anywhere." Then he asked the mob to leave since Thompson was not there. But they were too hot for some abolitionist's blood. Finally, the mayor ordered the ladies to go, saying he could not protect them any longer. They filed out to a member's house nearby where they could continue their meeting. Now the mob shifted its target: "Garrison! Garrison! Out with him! Lynch him!" They found the editor, and led him through the streets with a rope around his neck, his clothing half-torn from his body, and thousands standing on the side to jeer. Garrison showed no fear; he was calm and kept asking only for five minutes to address the mob. The mayor rescued him by ringing him with deputies and carrying him off to jail for safe-keeping, and the mob dispersed. The next morning he was let out, and went off to recover from the experience. Two weeks later he was back at the Liberator, and Thompson was off to England.

Several of the Boston papers had helped whip up the lynch spirit, but now they deplored the grim effect of their own editorials. The use of violence was bad, they said, and a grave danger to free speech.

The bravery of the women under threats of mobs gave heart to others less bold. They had given to freedom a more useful service than any of us, Dr. Channing said. "The defenders of freedom are not those who claim and exercise rights which no one assails, or who wins shouts of applause by well-turned compliments to liberty in the days of her triumph. They are those who stand up for rights which mobs, conspiracies, or single tyrants put in jeopardy; who contend for liberty in that particular form which is threatened at the moment by the many or the few. To the abolitionists this honor belongs."

6 ❧ The Case of the Slave Child Med

In the fall of "the mob year," the abolitionists made plans to send David and Maria to England on a special mission. By now both were giving all their talents and energies to the cause. David had done great service with a series of public letters on slavery and the slave trade, addressed to a prominent English philanthropist. He had gone down to Washington to urge support for the anti-slavery petitions which had begun to pour into Congress. In Boston, Maria helped raise funds to establish a home for orphaned Negro children, and in New Rochelle, she started a neighborhood effort to desegregate a small school.

She visited the Female Anti-slavery Society in Philadelphia to suggest they develop closer relations with the abolitionist women of both Britain and Boston. It was probably in the homes of Robert Purveys and James Forten, the wealthy Negro abolitionists, that she talked with many runaway slaves whose accounts of their lives in bondage roused her to very "unchristian" anger. She met James and Lucretia Mott, too, the Quaker abolitionists. From Mrs. Mott she must have heard the story of how, a few years earlier, when the Philadelphia women had called a meeting to begin their society, they could find no woman capable of taking their chair. So they had asked James McCrummell, a Negro friend, to help them. "You know at that time, and even to the present day," Mrs. Mott said, "Negros, idiots, and women were in legal documents classed together, so that we were very glad to get one of our own class to come and aid us in forming that society."

Despite the fact that Maria undertook such missions as this, she never liked female conventions and societies that separated women from men. "They always seemed to me like half a pair of scissors," she said. She paid her dues, however, attended the meetings, made things for their benefit sales, and saw they did great good. But she thought they exerted stronger influence in behalf of women's freedom than of the slaves'.

No matter what her doubts on this score, she could not stand people who ridiculed those "silly women" and "petticoat politicians" for tampering with the slavery issue. She would fire back the anecdote about the time Napoleon told a French lady that he did not like to hear women talk politics, and the lady replied: "Sire, in a country where women are beheaded, it is very natural that they should like to know the reason."

"And where women are brutalized, scourged, and sold," said Maria, "shall we not inquire the reason?"

In Maria's letters she spoke several times of the hoped-for expedition to England, but nothing seemed to come of it. Then a plan to go to Mexico took shape—to join Benjamin Lint in starting a settlement there to be based upon free, not slave, labor—but that too faded off as talk of war with Mexico rose. Again she and David resolved to go to England. From London George Thompson wrote that the abolitionists there were determined to have David edit a new periodical they were about to establish. But the promised financial backing vanished.

"Of many changes there is no end!" Maria wrote a friend at this point. David was plainly having great trouble. His newspaper editorship ended in a lawsuit which harried him for years, once even causing his arrest. His law practice disappeared. He thought of moving out to new western lands in Illinois, or of going to New York to edit the Emancipator. But the plans went awry, hopes faded, promises failed. In the summer of 1836, when tasks separated them briefly, the letters between them revealed how anguished David was by repeated

disappointments, and how lovingly Maria comforted
and strengthened him.

"Few men in the world have done more good than you
have done," she wrote. "Few are more truly respected.
God knows that I consider my union with you His richest
blessing. It has made me a better and a happier woman
than I ever was before. I had rather be your wife without a cent in the world, than to possess millions and not
be your wife. I have deep reason to say and feel this, for
you have been to me a most kind, considerate and forgiv-
ing husband, and I have ever loved and respected you
with my whole heart. How many times have you guided
me when I was wrong! How many times have you
strengthened me when I have been weak! How often
restored me to my balance when I have been perverse and
unreasonable! If we can but live together, and you still
love me, I will not ask for more of this world's goods. *Do*
you still love me? God only knows how deeply and ten-
derly I love you; and how often the tears start to my eyes
because I cannot relieve your troubles."

In the midst of their own troubles they were caught up
in two fights of great importance. Toward the end of "the
mob year" Southern legislatures had launched moves to
clamp legal controls on the antislavery press. They peti-
tioned Northern states to make it a crime to print and
distribute literature "calculated to incite the slaves to insurrection and revolt."

In the North, some people welcomed these demands. The decision of one Boston judge had already shown agreement. The editor of the Boston *Courier* seized the chance to call for suppression of the *Liberator*. Another Bostonian even urged that abolition meetings be banned, too.

Debates in most Northern legislatures at first favored the slaveholders' point of view. But how could one constitutionally take away freedom of the press? The question did not bother Governor Edward Everett of Massachusetts. His 1836 message called antislavery agitation "an offense against the peace" and asked all citizens to stop talking abolitionism.

Indignantly, the abolitionists replied, "We can neither permit the gag to be thrust into our mouths by others, nor deem it the part of 'patriotism' to place it there ourselves. The more fiercely our rights are assailed, the closer we will hold them to our hearts."

Since the Whig Party had the votes to pass a gag law, the abolitionists called for a public hearing on the bills which might infringe on liberty of speech and press. Several abolitionists spoke at the March hearings, attended by many of the antislavery women. Garrison and others countered Southern claims that they meant to destroy the Union. Then William Goodell created an uproar when he charged that not the abolitionists but the Southern "slave power" was trying to "rob the free states of those liberties brought to Massachusetts by the Pilgrims and cherished by their descendants." The real question, he cried, was "one of *liberty and rights*—not *black,* but *white and black!*"

An irrepressible roar of agreement went up from the gallery and the chairman's gavel crashed the meeting abruptly to a close. But the Garrisonians had carried the day. The committee issued a report calling for calmness and toleration in discussion, but it asked for no gag laws. In all the other Northern states, too, the South's petition was turned down.

When warm weather came to Boston a few months later, with it arrived the usual summer visitors from the South. It was an old custom for the slaveholders to escape the humidity of their plantations and seek comfort near New England beaches. Usually they brought slaves with them to tend to their needs. Ever watchful for slaves eager to escape, the abolitionists, and especially the women, kept a close eye on the chief hotels favored by the Southerners. When the opening came, they would spirit away the slave and pass him from one friendly home to another until the owner would tire of the search and return South minus his valuable "property."

There were several such successful escapes that summer of 1836. But when a Boston newspaper published an advertisement asking readers to help find and return one of the fugitives, the abolitionists resolved to test the legality of such a move. Consulting lawyers and the law books, they found it laid down that "a slave, bought in one state, acquires no rights as a freeman by being brought into another." This, it struck the abolitionists, ran counter to the Massachusetts Bill of Rights. Shouldn't their state shelter any slave brought within its limits by a master?

The chance to test the law came early in August. At a meeting of the women's society, someone reported a Southern family had recently come up to Boston with a Negro child in their keeping, presumably a slave. Maria was delegated to find out the facts. She visited the family and, finding that the six-year-old girl Med was a slave, tried to persuade her mistress to leave her at the colored asylum. She failed, of course, but learned the mistress planned to take the little girl back south.

With this evidence in hand, Maria hurried to the abolitionist lawyers. They got a writ of habeas corpus ordering Med's mistress to bring herself with the child before a justice of the Massachusetts Supreme Court for a hearing on her condition.

The lawyers for the slaveholder did not deny in court that she intended to take Med back into slavery. But they also claimed that Southern masters had a legal right to hold human beings as slaves while they were visiting in free states. They even wept a little while pleading that the poor little slave might be separated from her slave mother in New Orleans if the court ruled out of mistaken benevolence. That pathos was marred when Ellis Gray Loring, arguing the abolitionist case, arose and proved that the mistress intended to sell Med on her way home, in order to pay the vacation expenses.

Chief Justice Lemuel Shaw ruled that if a slave is brought into a free state voluntarily by his master, the slave becomes free if he chooses to use the provisions of Massachusetts law. In Massachusetts, he said, "slavery cannot exist because it is contrary to natural right."

Many hailed the decision as one of the most important in half a century, and especially noteworthy because it was "obtained through female agency."

Maria smiled the next day to read in the *Commercial Gazette* that though the decision was unquestionably lawful, it "is much to be regretted; for such cases cannot but injure the custom of our hotels, now so liberally patronised by gentlemen from the South."

How to injure Southern business—business based upon slave labor—was at this very moment under discussion in abolitionist circles. Some raised the issue originally as a matter of personal responsibility. Could one's conscience permit one to buy and use the products of slave labor? Wasn't that giving support to slavery itself? After thinking prayerfully about it, some resolved to abstain. Maria was among them. "The sugar does not taste good," she said, "because it brings me the image of the toiling slave." Lucretia Mott carried a little paper bag filled with sugar for tea, to be sure of using a product of free labor. One fourteen-year-old girl on a visit to relatives reported: "I do not eat the products of slave labor but Aunt Rebecca has been very kind to me and has got me some other sugar. Once I was helping Aunt make some cake out of slave sugar and I got a little on my finger when without thinking I put it in my mouth, but spit it out, and I forgot myself once beside that."

A campaign was started to pledge people not to use slave labor products. The targets were the four staples of the slave states: cotton, rice, tobacco, and sugar. But not many took the pledge. Some abolitionists thought a boycott of this kind would divert too many from the central issue of abolitionism.

But there was another way to look at it. Why not engage in direct competition with slave labor? If Northern free labor could undersell Southern slave labor and take away the market, then it would cripple the South and reduce the value of the slaves. That would tend to make slavery worthless, and a burden the slaveholders would be glad to get rid of.

So ran the argument in the *Liberator*. Garrison appealed for abolitionists to try this "benevolent enterprise." He found a ready ear in David Child. France had reported that beet sugar could equal cane sugar production acre for acre. David wanted to prove that he could do that in America, and using free labor instead of slave labor.

This seemed a good opportunity to David. He could at last find anchorage in a project important to the antislavery cause. He worked up experimental plans and Maria wrote the wealthy abolitionist landowner Gerrit Smith to ask his help in raising $50,000 (offering security and interest) to buy land in Illinois and machinery to manufacture beet sugar on a large scale. But Smith turned her down.

Nevertheless, some money was obtained to send David to Europe to study beet sugar production in France, Belgium, and Germany. The parting would be difficult for Maria. She missed David badly even in brief separations but their devotion to the antislavery movement had already made them accept frequent and long absences. At the dock, just as he was about to board, David was arrested and jailed for an old debt. Maria was badly shaken but despite a fit of tears, managed to find friends who were able to pay the debt and get David released. He sailed in the fall of 1836, to be abroad for eighteen months.

Meanwhile, Maria arranged to stay with family or friends. Earlier that year, her new novel had appeared. *Philothea* was her attempt to return to a form she had not used for ten years. Set in ancient Greece, the novel contrasted two kinds of reformers: Aspasia, the coldly theoretical idealist who wants power, and Philothea, the generous, warm-hearted girl who appeals to human kindness to better the world.

Philothea deals with social reform and refers often to Greek slavery. It could easily be interpreted as applying to America. Yet critics who had disapproved strongly of

Maria's abolitionist writings welcomed the same theme set safely in another time and place. Even Sarah J. Hale, a leading editor of women's magazines—who had once accused Maria of "wasting her soul's wealth" in radicalism and "doing incalculable injury to humanity"—liked *Philothea*. The novel won popularity, going through three editions.

With David gone, Maria turned to grinding out short stories for newspapers and magazines to earn her keep, as she began work on another household service book, *The Family Nurse*. For company, she spent much time at the Lorings'. Ellis and Louisa Loring were among her closest friends. Although Mr. Loring was about her own age, she came to depend upon him almost as an older and wiser brother, quick to confide her inmost feelings and troubles to him and to seek his advice. He took care of all her contracts with publishers, received royalties for her, advanced her money to meet debts, and invested her savings.

Ellis Gray Loring was the kind of man who never let his social standing and prosperity keep him from antislavery work. He was the first lawyer in Boston to take a young Negro into his office and train him for the bar. He had made history with his successful plea for little Med's freedom and he was to defend many fugitive slaves during his career. The Lorings' daughter, Anna, now about seven, was one of Maria's favorites and the two exchanged many letters and visits throughout Maria's life.

A tendency to turn away from social life began to show itself in Maria. The Lorings were quick to notice it. Get out and mix with people of the world, they insisted, or you'll grow intolerant and cold. She knew there was much truth in it, so "I up and went," as she wrote a friend. She often went to Dr. Channing's, once getting him to sign his name at the head of a petition to abolish slavery in the District of Columbia. He was timid, and critical of abolitionism, but he liked Maria and she felt she "helped him a little."

The mainstay of the Boston Female Anti-slavery Society, Maria Chapman, was another friend Maria relied on now. Mrs. Chapman was the beautiful and witty wife of Henry Chapman, a wealthy merchant. (He and James Mott of Philadelphia were the only two businessmen Maria knew who discontinued business with the South because of their conscientious scruples about slavery.) Mrs. Chapman was a writer, often editing the *Liberator* in Garrison's absence and putting out the annual *Liberty Bell* volumes. Maria thought she was the most remarkable woman in the country, and was amused by her "real Christian hatred" for intriguers who might lower the standards of the cause.

Maria and Louisa Loring organized the first antislavery fair independently in 1834, and when it was adopted by the female society, Mrs. Chapman and her sisters became the chief managers. The "born duchess," as she was called, made the bazaars into fashionable affairs.

All kinds of merchandise were donated for sale, some coming from friends abroad. That winter Maria collected with great zeal prints and engravings of slavery, and bound them into a portfolio to sell at the fair. Sometimes only a few hundred dollars were raised; sometimes several thousands. The funds were never up to the great need, but somehow the abolitionists got their job done.

The sisters Angelina and Sarah Grimke became friends of Maria's at this time, too. They were of an aristocratic, slaveholding family in Charleston, South Carolina. Finding life in a slave society intolerable, they had broken away and moved to Philadelphia where they became Quakers and then abolitionists. In the fall of 1836 Garrison published Angelina's pamphlet, *An Appeal to the Christian Women of the South,* urging them to speak and act against slavery.

When the pamphlets reached Charleston in the mails they were seized and burned publicly, and the Grimkes were told their daughters would be jailed if they dared come home. Hesitantly at first, the sisters spoke to mixed audiences in parlors and churches, and then in crowded lecture halls in New York and Boston, braving the powerful prejudice against women. Wherever they gave their personal testimony on slavery, listeners' hearts were moved.

Many objections were soon raised to the "female orators." They were accused of being highly improper, especially when they spoke before "promiscuous assem-

blies" of men and women. The "woman question," some
abolitionists warned, would get mixed up with antislavery and throw that issue off the track.

But women like the Grimkes, Mrs. Chapman, and
Maria were not to be stopped. Before the year was out
they had gathered the signatures of 45,000 women to petitions against the slaveholders' plan to annex Texas. And
not long after, they had rounded up as many more signatures to do away with slavery in the District of Columbia.

Struggling for equality with men in the abolitionist
movement was a crucial step in the fight for women's
rights. But Maria knew you had to start earlier, with children. Girls form their character at an early period, she
said; they get their most important impressions when
they are young. If women are to win respect, attention,
and independence, they must see the world with clearer
eyes.

She concluded that "home education" was the best way
to reach women. But looking about, she found little that
could help do it. And so she had created the plan for the
Ladies' Family Library, a series of popular biographies of
outstanding women of the past. And again, as in her first
novels, she chose to write about the kind of women who
went to jail for their heretical opinions, women who
fought against tyrants, women who had wit, talent,
learning and a love for beauty which they tried to use to
good ends. All her heroines in her first three volumes

showed enthusiasm for liberty, hatred of oppression, and contempt for rank. And the actions of each one, as she tried to show, had some effect upon the character and destiny of her country. Every woman, she concluded, has the duty of doing whatever she can to lead her country on the right path.

Again drawing upon biography, she wrote a *History of the Condition of Women in Various Ages and Nations,* illustrating the ways in which women had been enslaved through the centuries.

Her *History* appeared as women began to complain that laws which kept them from owning or administering property—even property they had themselves earned or inherited—were outrageously unjust. The two volumes were bulging with facts and not easy to read, but they helped knock down man-made barriers to equal rights for women.

7 ❧ A Northampton Farm

As David's research in Europe neared its end, Maria's
spirits rose. There was talk again of an Illinois company
to carry out the beet sugar experiment. "I would prefer
staying near Boston," Maria said, "but I could be happy
anywhere, if only I could be with my dear husband, and
contribute to his happiness and prosperity."

But something went wrong with the Illinois project,
and when David returned, there was no place for him to
go. They were without work or money. The Lorings generously took them in. For four months they lived with
their friends, planning to pay for their room and board,

but rarely able to find the dollars for it. It was a bitter winter for Maria. "Poverty is a light thing to me," she wrote Louisa later, "but a sense of dependence on others is galling."

Maria's restless father, who had moved thirteen times in the twenty years since he had given up his bakery, had long been urging her to unite their households. She had doubted it could be a happy arrangement. But now Mr. Francis made an offer that seemed to meet their desperate needs. He would take $3,000 he had planned to leave her in his will, and spend it on a farm in Northampton, in western Massachusetts. He put up $1,000 for a hundred badly neglected acres, with no fences, a barn in ruins, and an old shanty with two little rooms and a low garret.

With the remaining $2,000 they would rebuild and repair, and Maria had a pleasant vision of a quiet rural home at last. So when winter ended, David went up ahead to whitewash the shanty and patch its holes, and Maria and her father soon followed. Sugar beet seeds arrived from France in the spring, and David was ready to begin his experiment. But Mr. Francis was already restless again, complaining of being away from old friends and family scenes. He was reluctant to part with more money, and without fences or a costly stone wall to protect the crop, their land was useless. David had to hire an acre, and together he and Maria planted it.

Maria got up at three or four in the morning, weeding for hours at a time. Often she worked into the night mending David's old clothes or making a new coat for him. At first it was fun to be on her own again, and she wrote the Lorings light and gay letters, teasing them about the lazy hours rich Bostonians kept.

But as the months wore on, their problems and labors multiplied. A year later, Maria was telling a friend, "I now have two oxen, two horses, one cow, two laborers, father and ourselves to look after." She cooked for them all, sewed quilts, knitted stockings, made stout woolen trousers for David and the two hired hands, pieced and lined blankets for the horses, sewed calico gowns and capes for the Irish servant woman, and on top of it all, had her father to cope with.

Mr. Francis was "a kind and good old man as ever lived," Maria had said. But living with him was another matter. "You can't know, you can't imagine," she confided to Louisa, "what we have had to suffer since we came into a pecuniary connection with father. The old gentleman meant to do us a kindness, but he is unacquainted with sentiment, and has a violent prejudice against literature, taste, and even the common forms of modern civilized life."

Her brother James had warned her she would never be able to stand living with their father. And he was right, Maria found. "It is enough to make one turn to drunkenness or suicide," she said. "Of all trials I ever met, this is the most intolerable."

David was like Job under this sorrow, miraculously patient and cheerful.

Northampton soon found out it had a literary celebrity

in town and the Childs were courted by the local society. "All goes smoothly between us and the grandees," Maria said, "until I bring the Anti-Slavery petitions between the wind and their nobility."

Evidently their abolitionism had not been left behind in Boston. Carrying around petitions was still "odious work," but "evening after evening," she reported, "David is battling it in taverns and stores." They grew discouraged, but they kept at it. They soon discovered the amount of prejudice against Negroes in Northampton was as great as elsewhere in the North. The many Southerners in the seminary for young ladies, as well as their headmistress, openly expressed sympathy for slavery. There were direct ties with slaveholders through a number of local citizens who had moved South and had acquired slaves or become overseers.

One local man married a Georgia lady rich in slaves and managed her large plantation. When they came to cool Northampton that summer Maria watched him parade the streets with two slaves walking behind him. One of the slaves, trained for the job, as Maria thought, would go into the stores and taverns to preach up the merits of slavery, telling how much she pitied and despised free Negroes who had to work so hard. The other slave appeared very unhappy and discontented and was vigilantly guarded.

The Northampton hotels were full of Southern travelers, attracted by the beautiful scenery of the Connecticut

River valley. The landlords had no love for abolitionists. One of them became very angry at David for asking a colored man if he were free. "I dislike slavery as much as you do," the landlord told David, "but then, I get my living by slaveholders."

Maria put all she knew about Southern influence in Northampton into a series of letters for Theodore Weld, the abolitionist, who was compiling his book, *Slavery As It Is: The Testimony of a Thousand Witnesses.* "Disgusting as the picture is," she concluded, "we are probably freer from the pollution than most large towns in New England, because little business is done here, and manufactories are small and few."

One of the patricians in pursuit of Maria was the wife of Judge Lyman. "The very embodiment of aristocracy," Maria said: "hates republics, hates democracy in every form, of course hates reforms of all sorts, and loves to have woman a graceful vine that droops and dies, unless it can find some stately oak around which to twine itself."

But Maria discovered Mrs. Lyman to be anything but a drooping vine herself, with noble impulses and "a brave, imprudent frankness." She liked her, despite her distorted views. "If she can manage to like me, it must be because she respects the daring freedom of speech which she practices."

They ran into trouble, however, when Mrs. Lyman tried to get Maria to make friends with a local slaveholder. It wasn't that María avoided talking with slaveholders. She even sought them out. She had many an hour's argument with them, and usually they liked her, though her principles seemed stern and uncompromising. She wasn't so intolerant that she could not see slaveholders as individual people, often with good qualities. But she also learned that "men who are true and honorable on all other subjects will twist, and turn, and deceive and say what they must absolutely know to be false on this subject."

What accounted for their inconsistency? She could only suppose that while conscience told them the system was wrong, its whisper wasn't strong enough to overcome the temptation of personal advantage.

Even more importantly, "by education and habit they had so long thought and spoken of the colored man as a mere article of property, that it is almost impossible for them to recognize him as a man, and reason concerning him as a brother, on equal terms with the rest of the human family."

Her argument touched the match to the question of whether slaveholding was a sin. Soon Maria was lending both Mrs. Lyman and the judge some books on abolitionism.

Around this time word spread that a visitor was coming up from Charleston with a slave who would prove how false and exaggerated abolitionist talk was. This slave was very much against freedom and detested the North, so the story ran. Maria accepted the challenge and when the family came, promptly wrote the mistress asking if it wasn't hypocrisy to bring on petted and indulged household slaves, who left children or other ties behind them, and then boast of them as loving slavery and as samples of the general condition of bondage. Of course the mistress was furious. She told her slave Rosa that Maria had insulted her.

The indignant Rosa came to Maria, who read her a copy of the letter and asked her to judge for herself. In half an hour they were the best of friends. The slave came back again and again to talk, and soon Maria was working out plans for Rosa to get her freedom.

But Rosa had left her children in Charleston. The struggle in her mind to choose between her children and her freedom was agonizing. At one point it seemed she would decide to remain in Massachusetts when a pathetic letter came from her daughter in slavery, begging her to come back. Maria said nothing to sway Rosa's mind, but merely assured her that she would be her friend and get a good home for her if she chose to take her freedom. At last Maria saw Rosa follow her mistress into the stagecoach that took her away from freedom. One slave-owning family boasted that Maria tried hard but could not coax Rosa away from her "beloved" mistress. "They must know this is untrue," said Maria, "but Christians that will steal will lie also."

And then, prophetically, she added, "I do not believe the South will voluntarily relinquish her slaves, so long as the world stands. It must come through violence. I would it might be averted, but I am convinced that it cannot be."

Not every moment was spent in hard labor. There were pleasant interludes, too. Maria's brother John and his family lived in nearby Springfield. Visiting them, she was brought a beautiful bunch of flowers by a young girl, a stranger, who said she had gathered them for the lady who years ago had told her such pleasant stories in the *Miscellany*. It was a small gesture, but Maria was moved by it, and so deeply that she suddenly realized how much she missed the applause and popularity she had known before she had chosen the antislavery side. She liked to tell herself success in that sense hadn't mattered, but now she knew it had.

Children always reached Maria's deepest feelings, yet she and David were never to have any of their own. A little while after the incident of the flowers, she wrote, "I never felt so forcibly as within the last year, that to a childless wife, life is almost untenanted."

Young John Sullivan Dwight, minister of the Unitarian church in Northampton, was another oasis. He was bashful and slender, and his head sang with so much Mozart and Haydn that he had trouble remembering his sermons. His preaching, Maria thought, gave off a mild, transparent, amber light. Later he was to become a founder of Brook Farm and the nation's leading music critic. Now he was salvation for Maria. He would drop by the beet farm to see her, and she would leave her work, sitting down with dirty gown and hands. In fifteen minutes their talk was "high up in the blue." She was ready to take a flight with him from the washtub or dishpan any time he would come along.

But she couldn't float out of Northampton on those stray balloons. The farm work never eased off as David ran into endless difficulties. Badly needed machinery rusted in New York because the money wasn't on hand to pay for shipment. Just when great speed was called for in production lest the product spoil, labor was short. David had to drag along with one man when he needed six.

Desperate to help, Maria tried to cover expenses by making some of the beet sugar into candy. Send me recipes, she wrote friends in Boston, I'll make bonbons, barley candy, rock candy, peppermints, anything!

Little came of that, evidently, for soon she was talking of trying for a teaching job in Boston during the winter. She was discouraged from writing fiction because it wouldn't pay; too many readers had refused to buy the novels of an abolitionist. Could anyone send her editing to do, or compiling, or map-coloring?

She did not blame David in any way. He was remarkable at mastering difficulties, and doing whatever he tried, she told a friend.

But his soul was almost wormed out of him by want of funds, and the delays caused by the breakdown of cheap machinery. Yet he did prove it was practical to make beet sugar in America. The trouble was, he could not do it on a scale large enough to make it a commercial success. He published a book on what his experiments had taught him. And he won a silver medal for his raw and refined sugar at one Massachusetts exhibition that year and a $100 award at another. He was too far ahead of his time. Fifty years later, beet sugar was to become a profitable American industry.

By the spring of 1839 Maria was praying that someone would open a sugar company in Boston and offer David a job. "I struggle terribly with home-sickness," she confessed to Louisa. If she could only escape from Northampton without being separated from David. But he had put so much time and money into the experiment and had so set his heart on giving it a fair trial that she could see no way out.

The times offered little promise for change. The effects of the great depression that had seized the country in 1837 were still being felt everywhere. You could see what it meant all through New England. Great businesses had collapsed, banks and factories had closed. In New York, every third working man was out of a job. Not money, but poverty, is the root of all evil, Maria wrote grimly to Louisa.

David returned from a brief stay in Boston to report that differences of opinion within the antislavery movement were growing deep and bitter. And Garrison was in the center of the storm. For a long time he had published such violent attacks on the "pro-slavery" church in the

Liberator that many of the abolitionists were filled with dismay. "Let other subjects alone until slavery is finished," they begged him. But he went on adding other causes to his columns. He had already alienated many with his support of woman's rights.

Now he came out for "universal emancipation of all humanity from all bondage to human government." Pacifism alone was not enough, he argued; since all governments base themselves upon military force, the true pacifist cannot recognize any government. Nonresistance must be our only weapon against Southern aggression, he said. Political action he repudiated outright. He was against voting, or holding office, or taking any part in the affairs of government.

Plainly, Garrison wanted perfection in this world. And he would adopt and promote through the *Liberator* any new or radical idea which in his opinion tended to that end. What he had come to stand for sounded like anarchy to many of the abolitionists. Unless he would stop mixing up woman's rights, nongovernment and perfectionism with the antislavery cause, he would drive supporters away and wreck the movement.

Garrison's defenders said he was not trying to shove his opinions down others' throats. He never said his ideas should be made a test for membership. He welcomed controversy, and insisted on open debate and free opinion. Maria and David joined Loring and Sewall and Phillips in supporting him. Maria regretted that on both sides of the controversy there was fierce excitement and exaggerated suspicion. The quarrel "makes me sick at heart, discouraged, and ashamed," she wrote. But she could not avoid being drawn in. She traveled to Boston for the Female Anti-slavery Society convention, and, when a split took place, she sided with Mrs. Chapman and the other Garrisonians and presided over the first meeting of the reorganized body.

A month later came the crucial annual meeting of the American Antislavery Society. The opposing sides were heading for a collision over the woman question and the political question. A few weeks before the meeting the Liberty Party was formed by the politically-minded abolitionists, and James Birney nominated for President. "Presumptuous folly," Garrison snorted. He organized a boatload of delegates from New England, the majority of them women, and shipped them down to the national meeting in New York. He promptly had Abby Kelly put on the business committee, to serve with men. Crying this was "contrary to the usages of civilized society," those who opposed it withdrew to form their own organization. Left in full control, the Garrisonians elected Lydia Maria Child, Lucretia Mott, and Maria Chapman to the executive committee. And still determined to keep abolitionism a moral crusade, they voted down political action. To promote their program, a new organ, the *National Anti-Slavery Standard,* was started in New York.

Maria returned to Northampton. Another year went by

in the dull round of cooking, washing, and scouring, with David working day and night on his beets. They were alone in the shanty now. Her father had become unbearable. He had even told the neighbors he had given up so much for this daughter that he had deprived himself of a home. That was too much for Maria. She and David agreed the old man must be left free to live where he liked. So again he wandered off, to take a house near Boston, leaving them under a load of debts they had contracted upon promises he failed to keep.

Money was owed to the workmen, too, and this troubled Maria the most. She was ready to do anything to pay up their debts. Just then came appeals from Garrison that David come to New York to edit the *Standard* for $1,000 a year. It was only staggering along, he said; its very existence depended on getting his help.

But how could David go? It would mean giving up the farm and the beet experiment altogether, just when all the labor he had put into preparing the land and getting the equipment might be made to pay. No, tempting as the promise of a salary appeared, Maria could not bear to have David give up the experiment now. Perhaps it would become profitable enough to give them a modest living in the future, and the quiet home which was all she asked. So the answer was no.

But Garrison would not be turned down. Would Maria herself take the editor's job?

8 ⛓ Abolitionist Editor

Editing the *Standard* was a job Maria accepted reluctantly. She simply could not afford to say no. True, she had yearned to escape from the dreary Northampton farm, but not without David, and not to become embroiled in the organizational quarrels of abolitionism. Nor had she sought the job because to become the first woman editor of a newspaper might advance the cause of woman's rights. She felt no such noble motives. She and her husband were desperately in debt; if she could save enough of her salary, they could start over again.

Nevertheless, Maria seemed the perfect choice for the job. It was important that the Garrisonians have their own newspaper in New York. Someone with editorial skill, vision, and the diplomatic ability to heal the breach was needed in the post. Who better than Maria? Her literary reputation would be a great asset, and besides, Garrison relished the chance to put a woman in the key position.

She shed bitter tears when she left David that May in 1841. It took courage to leave her home and go alone to New York, taking up a responsible job in a field few women had dared enter. Coming into the noisy, crowded city she felt dreadfully lonesome and forlorn. It had been arranged that she should have a room in the Eldridge Street house of Isaac T. Hopper, the venerable antislavery Quaker who was the business manager for the *Standard*. That helped a great deal, for she felt "as comfortable as a poodle on a Wilton rug" at the Hoppers'. She had a cheerful, sunny room, a good stove, a rocking chair, a few attractive pictures on her wall, and a borrowed music box on the mantelpiece. Looking down at the cobbled streets she missed the garden she had left in bloom. "Write me your thoughts in the fields and woods," she implored a friend. "If you don't, you have no business to have the woods. I like living among the bricks," she added; "it gives one such a marvelous delight in a glimpse of the fields."

She did not quite realize what an almost impossible task had been given her. The split at the 1840 convention had left the American Antislavery Society badly crippled. Almost all it had left were its principles. Funds had faded away, and membership had dwindled to the point where it was hard to find even a few stout souls for the executive committee. The *Standard* had been started without a subscriber and without a dollar.

Maria had turned newspaper editor just as a revolution in journalism was in the making. Since old Ben Franklin's days, newspapers had changed very little. It was almost a mistake to call them that, for they had little that was recognizable as real news—news that had happened today, yesterday, or even a week ago. The four-page sheets were poorly printed. The large, clumsy pages were a hodgepodge of market reports, ship movements, and odd paragraphs snipped from other papers. Sermons and speeches were quoted at interminable length—and long after they were delivered. Poems and serialized novels took up what space was left after the editor had unloaded his usually vitriolic political opinions upon his readers.

Reporters were nonexistent. Nobody went anywhere to get the news. There were no press associations, no sports pages, no features. Most of the newspapers were owned by one man, and he often doubled as editor and printer.

Not long before Maria's arrival the New York *Post* had come up with the radical idea of putting out a daily paper priced at just one cent—so everybody could afford it—and of bringing it to them on the streets through newsboys, instead of selling it over a counter. Going the *Post* one

better, the *Sun* decided to drop serious news altogether
and appeal to the broadest public with scandals, miracles,
and horrors. Next, James Gordon Bennett of the *Herald*
invented the interview and sent reporters into the streets
and offices and shops to look at the human scene and
describe it. It was a great step forward except that he was
interested only in the sensational. A month before Maria
took over the *Standard,* Horace Greeley had come on the
stage with his own penny daily, the *Tribune.* He was
using all the new techniques of journalism, but with a
special purpose: "to advance the interests of the people,
and to promote their Moral, Political and Social well-
being."

The *Standard* had no capital to invest in new methods
of journalism, and no staff but Maria. It had a special
purpose, too: to serve the antislavery movement.

In her first statement to her readers Maria announced:
"Such as I am, I am here—ready to work according to my
conscience and my ability; providing nothing but diligence and fidelity; refusing the shadow of a fetter on my
free expression of opinion from any man or body of
men; and equally careful to respect the freedom of
others, whether as individuals or societies."

After just two issues, Maria was confiding to Ellis
Loring: "How the *Standard* is going to be supported, I
know not. They are in debt for the printing and paper of
the last two weeks, and no money comes in." James

Gibbons, married to Hopper's daughter Abby, printed the paper and he had mortgaged his household furniture to keep the *Standard* going.

Maria and David (he was to send political articles from Northampton) were promised a joint salary of $1,000 a year. But at the end of the first three months she had been paid only $20, and in the next three received only $300 more. She was barely able to pay Friend Isaac her board, let alone send any money to David.

Worrying about how to keep the paper and herself alive, she nevertheless got on with the job. She planned each week's edition by herself. She had to read the other antislavery newspapers to keep track of developments elsewhere. She went to the meetings that promised to make news, wrote letters to ask for contributions, answered mail from readers. All this on top of the job of selecting what to print, writing the editorials, and rewriting and condensing communications abolitionists sent in from all over. She found the editing much more of a chore than she had expected: "The type is fine, and that large sheet swallows an incredible amount of matter." The cry was always "More! More!"

Suggestions and pressure came from all sides. No matter how wrong or foolish they were, she had to try to please all those who were interested in the cause. She had "an increasingly uncomfortable sense of being fettered by being the organ of a *society*. I am not certain whether one *can* fill such a position without injury to his own soul."

She and David picked editorial subjects that suited each one's own tastes and interests. Maria would tackle the woman question or capital punishment while David might handle the Florida war, the Texas question, or the tariff.

A typical issue showed a remarkable range of material. She got Isaac Hopper to write "Tales of Oppression," a series of pieces about his experiences as a social reformer. She reprinted slave ads from the Washington press. She ran letters from the South showing the effect of slavery on the master's moral conduct; news from British abolitionist organizations; a reprint from the *Dial* of Emerson's "Man the Reformer"; a long review of Harriet Martineau's novel about Toussaint; news from Washington of the debate on the gag law; a report from Nantucket about the fight to prevent the exclusion of a Negro girl from the high school; the personal account of a fugitive slave; and her own "ABC of Abolitionism for those who have not examined the subject."

Still, those four large pages seemed to yawn ever wider for more material. In her letters to her Boston friends Maria would scrawl in the margins requests for "any little incident on slavery or the general topic of freedom" they had run across, north, east, south or west. Or if they found anything especially interesting in their reading, would they just cite the chapter and verse?

As the only woman editing a newspaper, she was conscious that many eyes were glued to her performance.

"You may well suppose," she said, "that a woman is obliged to take more pains than a man would do, in order to avoid any inaccuracy or oversight in *state affairs.*"

There was a domestic aspect, too. In addition to the work men editors had, she was obliged to do her own washing and ironing, mending and making, besides frequent stitches for her husband's comfort.

A few months of this, and it seemed almost too much to bear. "How I do long to get out of this infernal treadmill!" she wrote Ellis Loring. "How I do long to be reunited to my dear husband, and have some quiet, domestic days again! It makes me groan to think that only four months of the stipulated year have passed." Nothing but David's money troubles would keep her another month, she said. "I hate it, with an inconceivable and growing hatred. Out of it I *will* get, by hook or by crook. I question the morality of letting one's soul thus be ground up, for a cursed reform! Excuse the word—nothing else would express my feelings."

Then, immediately: "I feel better now; what I have written answers for a sort of safety-valve."

In those early months she sometimes went to bed crying, and could not be comforted even by the Hoppers, who brought her peaches and melons, and assured her she was doing an incalculable amount of good to the antislavery cause.

Two months later, however, her mood was quite different. To Ellis she now wrote, "The ruling idea of my life is to make the *Standard* a first rate paper, and you *must* help me—both with counsel and communications. It is a lucky accident, that by serving me, you may likewise serve the cause of freedom."

She hungered for letters from friends. "Sitting alone in my chamber, a complete recluse in this vast city, I get run down and need an encouraging voice to wind me up, at least once a week." That week she heard from Gerrit Smith, the upstate philanthropist, who sent $20 toward her salary and said he was reading every issue thoroughly and was "delighted with the ability that sustained it, and the kind spirit that breathed through it."

David, too, wrote her that he liked the work she was doing. "I wonder you do," she replied, "for everything I write comes out with wrench and screw." But she could add that the Boston and Philadelphia abolitionists had also said—if they spoke sincerely—that they were "much satisfied."

In November she raised $25 somehow and, putting the *Standard* in Gibbons' hands, went up to Northampton to spend four weeks with David. The visit was one of almost unmixed pain, for David looked so thin and overworked that she hardly knew him. She found so many things to do for him that she did not have time for a single walk, or even to go out and look at the calves. As she made things more comfortable, his health and spirits mended astonishingly. She arranged to send up a woman to cook and wash for him, and they made plans once more for the time when their separation would end. Now she knew more than ever that she could not live without being loved. "What has wealth or fame to offer, compared with someone who thinks you the wisest, best, handsomest, and above all, the dearest person in the world?"

Back at her desk, Maria soon felt again the pressure of the quarrel over political action dividing the abolitionists. More and more, the rank and file were thinking that only united political action could rid the country of slavery. But Garrison's "no government" position barred politics as sinful and corrupting. Maria felt the same way. "I hate the contamination of political trickery," she said.

But all around her abolitionists were getting deeper and deeper into Liberty Party politics. Half a dozen antislavery congressmen had appeared in Washington and about thirty-five antislavery newspapers had sprung up around the country which either favored Liberty Party action or at least did not oppose it.

And "all around the board," Maria wrote Mrs. Chapman, "they want to cajole me into saying at least half a word, or allowing half a word to be said, in favor of third party to the readers of the *Standard*. Not as you knows on, says I."

She stood firm even when such close friends as Louisa Loring began to change their minds. "Her gentle spirit will soon make her disgusted with it," Maria commented. Perhaps she was against political action because women weren't allowed to go to the polls, someone suggested.

She replied that while she thought they had as good a right there as men, "politics rest on such a thoroughly bad foundation that I, for one, should feel no inclination to use the right."

As editor, her policy was neither to attack political action nor to support it. Here the old question of her responsibility to the organization came up. She meant to edit the *Standard* "conscientiously, according to *my* views of the good of the Society," she told Ellis Loring. Perhaps it was true that she wasn't following the counsel of the more fiery spirits in Boston, but the fact was, she said, so many different kinds of advice were being urged upon her that "I have found the absolute *necessity* of relying upon my own judgement. Had I done otherwise, I should have shifted about without rudder or compass."

The truth was, the American Antislavery Society no longer had any influence on the state groups and their auxiliaries. The spirit of the old crusade was still there, and through the tongues of Garrison and Phillips it was still recruiting abolitionists. But as fast as they were converted, they ran right into the Liberty Party.

Seeing this, Maria felt her way of editing the *Standard*, by appealing to reason and good feeling, would reach more widely among the people "and make a great many more half-abolitionists, and three-quarter abolitionists," than to make the paper a sounding board for noisy quarrels and vindictive name-calling. She wanted to cut through all political and religious differences and keep the *Standard* a family paper, appealing to young and old, the literary and the uneducated.

She was much too cool and philosophic for Garrison. And Maria sensed it. "The conviction that the paper needs a *man* at the helm in these days of Liberty Party and clashing with sects, is too strong to be mistaken," she wrote Ellis. But "*my* course I will not change for king or kaiser. I dictate to no one, but myself. Personal or party controversy shall *not* enter the *Standard* while I have charge. If they want fighting, let them change their editor—the sooner the better."

Soon the quarrels threatened to engulf Maria. Mrs. Chapman was hinting that Maria loved popularity too much, and was trying to please her *own* public. And Abby Kelly charged her with "disgracing and degrading" the *Standard*. She felt she was now in a false position. The Society had an undoubted right to decide what sort of paper it wanted, she said, and to hire an editor who in freedom of conscience could do the work it wanted done.

"But," she cautioned wisely, "they ought to have sense enough to be aware that they cannot have a paper to fight with abolitionists of all stamps but their own, and at the same time to find its way *generally* among the people. If they make the *Standard* like the *Liberator,* it will, like the *Liberator,* repel all but a limited number."

She had Wendell Phillips' testimony for it, too: "Know that all classes here, the ultra, the moderate, the half-converted, the zealous, the indifferent, the active, all welcome the *Standard,* and that it is fast changing them all into its own likeness of sound, liberal, generous, active, devoted men and women, without partiality and without hypocrisy—without shame—sifting out and building up —making a way for itself where no path was open before . . . ."

And she had the facts behind her, for the *Liberator* never reached more than 2,500 subscribers, while Maria in two short years had built the *Standard* to twice that number. One novelty in journalism that Maria herself introduced had helped to draw in many new readers.

9   The Streets of New York

Soon after Maria's arrival in the city, she had started to write a newspaper column for the Boston *Courier,* calling it "Letters from New York." The column proved so popular that she used it in the *Standard,* too. The personal pattern for newspaper correspondence which she set was soon taken up by other publications.

Maria, of course, could never be content with pictorial description of life in "the metropolis of America." She had a point of view on what she saw and it made trouble when she decided to prepare a book based upon her impressions of New York. Publishers were afraid of its "reforming character," they said, so she was obliged to put out the book herself. In spite of her fear of going deeper into debt, she took a chance and borrowed money from friends to pay for paper, printing, and binding. She relied on Ellis Loring's criticism in choosing and editing her columns for the book.

Letters from New York delighted its readers. Emerson's *Dial* called the *Letters* a "contribution to American literature, recording in a generous spirit, and with lively truth, the pulsations of one great center of existence." In less than a year two editions were sold out. "The great popularity of that volume surprises me," Maria said, "for it is full of ultraisms. However, there is always a sort of fascination about whatever gives out *itself* freely."

And that was how she gave herself to New York. It was a noisy, brutal town she came to in 1841. "This great Babylon," she called it, with its "magnificence and mud, finery and filth, diamonds and dirt, bullion and brass." She never forgot her first impression, pulling into the landing at early dawn in fog and drizzling rain, and close beside her a boat called the *Fairy Queen* laden with dead hogs.

The broad wharves she stepped on were piled high with barrels and boxes, sacks and bales, hampers and hogsheads. Bowsprits overhung the footways and masts and steeples punctuated the sky. The streets were a jumble of wood, brick and stone houses. Sails and flags flapped in the wind and gaudy signboards called from shop and tavern doors.

And noise—everywhere. The whistling steam ferries, chimney sweeps crying their services, newsboys hawking the penny papers, the oystermen's horns, the bells on the ragmen's carts, a wandering musician shrilling his bagpipe. "Hot corn! hot corn! Lily white corn! Buy my lily white corn!" Locksmiths and fruit vendors. And up and down the four cobbled miles of wide Broadway clattered the omnibuses and gigs and phaetons and tilburies and hackney cabs. In the gutters, the black gutters, pigs uglier than their ugly kind, rooting and snorting and stinking.

In 1841 this busiest and wealthiest of all cities boasted 300,000 inhabitants. But amid these masses Maria felt alone, lonelier than in the solitude of the forest. In many months of walking the crowded streets she saw only two faces she had ever seen before.

And the contrasts: "Wealth dozes on damask couches," Maria wrote, "while poverty camps on the dirty pavement. There, amid the splendor of Broadway, sits the blind Negro beggar, with horny hands and tattered garments, while opposite to him stands the stately mansion of the slave trader."

Maria enjoyed riding from the cool Battery and its newly planted groves of trees along the Bowery to Bloomingdale in the north. It was a pleasant road, much used for fashionable drives. The town limits stretched much farther but the street maps ended at Twenty-third Street. Beyond were the rural places where the rich summered— Murray Hill, Bloomingdale, Harlem.

The wealthy people had moved up from the tip of Manhattan and built their double houses near City Hall. A few elegant mansions had begun to appear as far north as lower Fifth Avenue and Washington Square, which had once been a pauper's burial ground. Those who preferred hotel life wintered in their suites at the Astor House and summered in their villas on the Hudson.

Battery Park was Maria's favorite place, but she liked Union Park, too, with its circle of hedge, its well-rolled gravel walks, and its velvet greensward, "shaven as smooth as a Quaker beau." Its trim design was a rare and welcome contrast to the confusion of the city around it. St. John's Park, too, was a refuge—but from outside its gate. Maria resented that it was open only to the few genteel people who held its keys.

Here and there in the town were small garden spots, where she could eat an ice cream in shaded alcoves of latticework. You Bostonians, she chided them, have nothing like this; you would think it too vulgar.

For free entertainment there were countless parades. One day Maria stood by to watch the two-mile-long procession of the Washington Temperance Society. All classes and trades were represented, with music and banners. "Troops of boys carried little wells, and pumps," she reported in her column, "and on many of the banners were flowing fountains and running brooks. One represented a wife kneeling in gratitude for a husband restored to her and himself; on another, a group of children were joyfully embracing the knees of a reformed father. Fire companies were there with badges and engines; and military companies, with gaudy colors and tinsel trappings."

Toward the end came carriages bearing the six men who had started the anti-drinking society: a carpenter, a coach-maker, a tailor, a blacksmith, a wheelwright, and a silver-plater.

Maria felt no superiority toward the human wrecks she saw everywhere in the streets. "They excite in me more of compassion than dislike." God alone knew, she said, "whether I should not have been as they are, with the same neglected childhood, the same vicious examples, the same overpowering temptation of misery and want."

In her columns she tried to teach society that "it makes its own criminals, and then, at prodigious loss of time, money, and morals, punishes it own work."

She preferred not to put too many disagreeable things in her column. But sometimes she saw such outrages she could not help speaking of them. In her first summer in New York she learned that almost fifteen hundred dogs had been killed; in the hottest weather, three hundred were slaughtered in one day. The company of dog-killers hired by the city were a frightful sight, with their bloody clubs and spattered garments. They knocked the poor animals to the pavement and beat them to death. People had to be protected against the packs of stray dogs, but Maria protested the cruel and demoralizing way it was done.

From Maria's window in the Hopper house she could see a tiny patch of garden, trimly kept and neatly whitewashed. In the absence of country brooks and blooming laurel, she was thankful for its marigolds and poppies. Two beautiful young trees, an ailanthus and a catalpa, stood just beside her brick wall.

They too would worship two little trees and a sunflower, she told her readers, "if you had gone with me to the neighborhood of the Five Points the other day." It was on a warm afternoon, and the slum dwellers had not yet been driven indoors by darkness and the police. The air she breathed was like an open tomb. Thievery, prostitution, murder—she saw nearly every form of human misery, every sign of human degradation.

It struck her as a sad irony that where the slums of the Five Points now stood, there was once a spacious pond of sweet, soft water which could have supplied half the city's needs. But it was filled in at incredible expense, with a million loads of earth. And now the city had to get its water from a great distance by the vast expense of the Croton Water Works. "Thus," she commented, "does society choke up nature, and then seek to protect itself from the result, by the incalculable expense of bolts, bars, and gallows, watch-houses, police courts, constables, and prisons. Satan might well laugh at the shortsightedness of the world, all the while toiling to build the edifice it thinks it is demolishing."

Maria's travels about the town were usually taken with

Isaac Hopper's son John. The young lawyer, fifteen years her junior, was very un-Quakerish in his lively wit and his delight in the theater. Something about him reminded Maria of David, and she treated him like a son. But unlike David, he could be counted on for sensible advice in practical affairs. She came to lean on him so heavily she felt lost without him.

Together they explored not only the city but the beautiful places on its edges. For six cents they could exchange the hot and dusty streets for Staten Island or Jersey; three cents would take them to Brooklyn, and a half-cent pay for a delightful sail of ten miles to Fort Lee.

Across the Hudson was Hoboken, a charming summer resort popular for its grand view of the city, and the bay with its islands, fortifications, and shipping. One spring Maria found two tents of Indians camped on the river's edge, and when she talked to them discovered they belonged to the Penobscot tribe she had known on the shores of the Kennebec during her years in Maine.

From Hoboken she and John walked three miles on the river path to Weehawken, where Hamilton had fought his fatal duel with Burr in 1804. They returned to the city by boat, in the moonlight, to find rockets rising from Castle Garden and dropping their blazing jewels on the bay.

In the autumn, Maria visited the synagogue on Crosby Street to see the Jewish New Year festival and listen to the services chanted in Hebrew. It was the oldest of the five congregations established by the city's ten thousand Jews.

New York's shipyards could not be overlooked, and Maria spent many hours watching vessels built. The most graceful ship she ever saw was a slaver, a Baltimore clipper called the *Catharine,* taken by British cruisers and brought into New York with all her chains and padlocks to be condemned by a United States court and sold. The city, she knew, was secretly much involved in the slave trade.

Once she boarded the French frigate *Belle Poule,* which had carried the remains of Napoleon from St. Helena to France, and listened to a concert by the same band which had attended the body. She saw the steam frigate *Kamchatka,* built in the Brooklyn Navy Yard for the Czar, sail out for Kronstadt, and felt proud that great foreign powers sent to this young country when they most wanted ingenious machinery or skillful workmanship.

When Maria wanted to escape from the never-ending scrabble in the streets and shops, she would lounge an hour or two in the gallery of the American Art Union on Broadway. It had been founded in 1840 to spread engravings of paintings to a wide public who could not afford the prices of the originals. About fifteen hundred people were paying five dollars a year for membership, most of them scattered all over the country. With the money taken in, the Union bought and exhibited the work of young artists, and established painters, too. Once a year a lottery was held, with the winners getting the original paintings and everyone else at least an engraving.

When the reader wondered at an abolitionist's interest in art and artists, Maria replied: "I *am* a reformer, but please henceforth never to think of me thus. If anti-slavery made me take one particle less of interest in the sad music of the moon, the birth and death of the flowers, and above all, in the rosecolored dreams of youthful love, I would abjure it tomorrow, even at the risk of the Calvinistic hell for my disobedience to my conscience."

She befriended many young artists, writers, and musicians, who found she not only understood what they were trying to do but was always ready to give them practical help. There was the painter William Page, for instance. She stood by him through several financial and marital crises, and finally helped to raise the money to send him to Florence to study and work. Later Page became president of the National Academy of Design.

She seldom fell victim to hero worship, but to the New York concerts of the Norwegian violinist Ole Bull she reacted with the fervor of a schoolgirl. She managed to get his picture to hang on her wall, and when she overcame her shyness and finally met him, they became fast friends. He would seek the quiet of her parlor to practice and compose, and when he left a violin string there, she wove a wreath on it.

She studied music, too, piling her desk high with its histories and dictionaries, trying to learn something of its science. "But though the books tell me something," she said, "they do not tell me half as much as music itself."

When she felt depressed and discouraged, she wrote, "music gives a fresh impulse to my soul, kindles in me a new life." Ole Bull's playing always made her feel she wanted to produce something as beautiful in her own work. She doubted she ever could, but she was sure she would write much better after knowing the intense pleasure she experienced in his music. "I am violin-mad," she confessed; "no other instrument seems to me so like the human soul—when a human soul really breathes through it."

Lionized by Europe and America, Bull sometimes treated such friends as Maria with indifference or coldness. Still, she cherished him. And it did not lessen her interest in other artists. To her young friend Abby Hutchinson, rising to great popularity with her family, the Hutchinson singers, she once wrote this advice: "Dare to trust your own nature; and while you make no war upon the world and its conventionalities, have courage to act and think quietly at variance with its spirit and its customs. Do not let the world spoil you. I pray God that you may preserve your simplicity."

Maria's greatest pleasure came from music, and New York had much to offer. There was the Philharmonic, which gave four concerts a year, and the Italian Opera. On summer evenings one could stop by for refreshments at the Alhambra Café on Broadway, and watch the fountain while listening to the orchestra. Or one could go down to Castle Garden for the brass band, and sit in the

Battery breeze, watching the ships in the bay. One of the most popular orchestras was at Niblo's where one stepped off dusty Broadway into a fairyland garden, with brilliant lights, fountains, and oriental shrubbery.

There were four theaters in New York then, none of them fashionable, Maria said, though the Park Theatre had a lingering gentility. The Bowery Theatre went in for "gorgeous decorations, fantastic tricks, terrific ascensions, and performances full of fire, blood, and thunder." In the pit there was always a crowd that tried to assist the play with improvised lines, action, and sometimes battles livelier than any on stage.

The most popular entertainer of all was P. T. Barnum, "a genuine Yankee for contrivance and perseverance," Maria said. At his American Museum on Broadway, just half a block from the printshop where Greeley had launched his *Tribune,* he exhibited monstrosities the crowds thronged to see: dwarfs, giants, double-headed calves, freaks of nature and freaks of his imagination— "all the old characters that walk like steam engines, buzz like mosquitoes, and have mouths like a ribbon-loom." When one stopped to think what an important part popular amusement played in the education of the people, Maria wrote, "this ingenious prodigality of grotesqueness becomes somewhat serious." A bored and dull audience, without standards of taste, eager for fun and laughter, submitted to this Connecticut Yankee's practical jokes on a grand scale.

Maria found her column useful in winning support for the work of Isaac Hopper, who had left his antislavery job to organize a Society for the Reform of Prisons and Their Inmates. Hopper had for many years been an inspector of the Philadelphia prison where he had come to realize that the system of tormenting criminals into what was called "good behavior" could never work. Something better than fear must be appealed to. By treating young prisoners as a kindly father, spending long hours in educating them, and finding jobs for them outside, Hopper had succeeded in rehabilitating many.

Maria visited Sing Sing Prison, thirty miles up the Hudson, to see what changes Hopper's ideas were bringing about. Sing Sing was trying to dispense altogether with physical punishment. Not long ago three thousand lashes with a cat-o-six-tails used to be inflicted in the course of a month. But they had found that "degraded as the prisoners were, they still had hearts that could be touched by kindness, consciences that might be aroused by appeals to reason, and aspirations for a better course of life which often needed only a voice of sympathy and hope to be strengthened into permanent reformation." Now the new system was to punish as sparingly as possible, and to give praise and more privileges for every indication of improvement. Music had been added to the recreation program, and the women were given flowers to keep in their cells. Let the wags laugh at the modern mode of curing crime by flowers and music, Maria wrote;

"experience has proved that love is the best controlling power."

Maria's warm sympathy for the suffering, and the details of their lives which she described in her *Letters* made them more than a new sensation in journalism. They did much, said one of her young readers—Thomas Wentworth Higginson, himself to become a noted reformer—to promote a fresh inquiry into the foundations of social science.

In the early 1840's, everyone seemed to have his own blueprint for reform. Maria's old Northampton friend, John Dwight, had left his pulpit and joined the Brook Farm experiment. Maria, too, was urged to become a member of the cooperative community.

She turned down the chance to join the Brook Farmers, however, for she had just had quite enough of hard work without pay on David's farm in Northampton. But she followed its course closely. "I have supposed it will fail," she said; "the beginnings of such things always do. But whether it succeeds or not I think it will do much good, for these plans are unquestionably the nucleus of a great idea, destined to work important social reforms."

Meanwhile, here on this imperfect island of Manhattan, imperfect people were trying every which way to have a perfectly wonderful time. Celebrating the holidays, for instance. The town greets the New Year in the same noisy style that she does everything else, Maria said in her column, with a great firing out of the old and a firing in of the new. Guns and pistols went off in the streets all night long. On January 1, the old Dutch custom was observed. No lady who *is* a lady will be out in the streets this day. She stays at home, dressed in her best, by her side a table covered with cakes, preserves, wines, oysters, hot coffee. As every gentleman is in honor bound to call on every lady he is still speaking to, the amount of eating and drinking is prodigious. The number of calls is a matter of pride and boasting among the ladies, and there is, of course, great rivalry in the magnificence and variety of the eating tables.

To furnish forth these feasts, the confectionery shops vie with each other. Ladies offer sugared gnomes, fairies, and mermaids, and cakes shaped into pyramids, obelisks, pagodas, towers and castles, topped by cooing doves and dancing cupids.

It was a great contrast to what Maria had seen on Christmas Day. Isaac Hopper—whose salary from the abolitionists was $200 a year—filled a large basket with cakes and, with Maria, went out into the most miserable streets to distribute them among hungry children. In one leaky, wind-racked tenement they visited they found fifteen families living without fire, sharing their knives and forks and loaning their bedclothes to the sick. Friend Isaac asked what each paid for his rent, and adding the sums together, found that the income from the wretched building in this filthy and crowded street was greater than the rent of many a Broadway mansion. "What does it say," Maria asked her readers, "concerning the structure of society on this Christmas day, nearly 2,000 years after the advent of Him who said, 'God is your father, and all ye are brethren?'"

The Fourth of July in New York was another holiday to be endured by those with sensitive ears. The big guns from the ships boomed majestically through the air, and crashing musketry, snapping pistols and spitfire crackers made it like a city besieged from dawn to midnight. Muskets were fired at the front doors and pistols from the windows. Rockets whiz into your bedchamber, said Maria, blazing grasshoppers jump at you on the sidewalk, and fiery serpents chase you across the streets. "From the alderman to the chimney-sweep, everyone lets go of his patriotism in gunpowder."

The city poured itself into the country, and the country, led by the same restless love of change and excitement, poured itself into the city. Farmers rushed in for noise and fun, and workmen rushed out for quiet and fresh air.

Though her ears hurt, Maria's eyes were rewarded. From every section of the city that night fireworks curtained the town with a tent of flame. Rockets with twining serpents, rockets with glittering meteors, rockets with metallic, many-colored stars, rockets with silver rain, rockets with golden rain, played and mingled in the air and were reflected in the rivers and bay. At Washington Parade Ground, at Niblo's and at Castle Garden, from private houses in every street, wheels, serpents and fountains went up from roofs and piazzas so that the entire city seemed on fire. (It was, in fact, at twelve different places that night.)

Wandering through the city, Maria thought that if the bells and the rockets, the guns and the orations added one particle to the love of liberty, they would not be a sham and a waste. Behind the fluttering, starry flag she could not help but see the fettered slave.

It was still but a short time since slavery had finally ended in New York. The last ten thousand slaves had been given their freedom in 1828. But even now there were New Yorkers who owned slaves in the South. The property of Southern planters was often bought by Northerners. One New Yorker owned twelve hundred slaves, and another three hundred. The great hotels—the Astor, the Metropolitan, the St. Nicholas—were filled with Southern planters and merchants. The newspapers advertised to Southerners the latest varieties of dry goods, boots and shoes, hardware. Many of the steamers and packets lining the wharves worked the coastal trade between the two regions, and were often owned jointly by Northerners and Southerners. The ships headed down the coast with clothing, hardware, fruit, liquor, butter, and cheese and came back up with cotton, tobacco, tar, turpentine, resin, pork, and molasses.

Yes, New York and the South were bound together by a thousand ties of commerce. And for the free Negro in the North, it meant another kind of chain: second-class citizenship. Maria observed that there was no segregation in housing in New York—nothing like the ghettoes which developed much later. Negroes lived in every ward of the city, distributed fairly evenly throughout. But though black and white were neighbors in their homes, what other freedom did the Negro have?

In only a few Northern states was he allowed to vote. Where did one see a Negro on a jury? In even the lowest public office? Training in a military company? He never rode the omnibus in New York. He entered only the lowest grogshop. He could not eat in any restaurant or oyster cellar that a white man went to, even if it was kept by one of his own people. There were scores of good hotels in the city but not one in which a Negro could find a bed. He might cook every meal and wait on every table, but he could eat only in the kitchen. He could be rich enough to buy out the whole theater but he could not sit in the boxes or pit. Only in the gallery, and, frequently, railed off from the whites.

In the churches he prayed in a "Negro pew," in the far corner of the gallery. If he was allowed to board a railway car, a steamer, or a stagecoach, he sat in a Jim Crow section. Wherever he went, whatever he did, the wall was there.

Even among many of the abolitionists, social mixing with Negroes was not done. In the New York women's antislavery society, Maria learned, Negroes were barred from membership. It seems the Mrs. Cox, who was "the very life and soul of the organization," insisted on the rule. While abolitionists attacked racial prejudice and backed the Negro's claim to full citizenship, they were sadly divided on consorting with Negroes socially. Some, of course, dared to flout the powerful and often dangerous prejudice of the period. And about these the more timid ones were always curious: "I hear that Mrs. Child has had a party lately, and invited colored persons," wrote one lady. "Do write and tell me about it!"

10 ⛓ Seeds of Truth

By the spring of 1843, Maria felt the hour had come for the parting between her and the antislavery organization. She could not be a cog in the organized machinery of reform. "From now on," she wrote Loring, "I will work in my own way, according to the light that is in me .... I never again will join *any* association, for *any* purpose."

In May she resigned from her post. The editorship was then offered to David. He took it, because there was no longer any reason to stay in Northampton. He had been forced to go into bankruptcy and to put up for auction whatever was left of the beet farm property.

He made clear to the American Antislavery Society that he insisted on full freedom to speak on all subjects connected with the abolitionist movement. And he said he had been in full agreement with his wife's conduct of the paper except that he would have permitted more controversy in its columns.

Maria did not really let go completely, despite her declarations. She helped David editorially, and when he went down to Washington now and then on behalf of the Massachusetts society, she took over.

But in financial matters, Maria resolved to separate her affairs entirely from David's. She made the necessary arrangements with Ellis, who handled her dealings with publishers. She wanted to remain in New York, no matter where David's experiments might take him. With this decision, a great load of anxiety was taken from her heart. She would do her best to keep David from any more entanglements, but there was no certainty she would succeed.

She loved David none the less for this; she simply knew their life together would be more secure if her earnings were kept in her own hands. That way there would be some money—however little—for them both to fall back upon if his ventures failed. He agreed to this step as a measure both necessary and just.

When Maria resigned from the *Standard,* she went on with her columns for the Boston newspapers (they were being copied in other papers, too, including Greeley's

Tribune), and returned to writing for children. In the next few years she published three small books in a series called *Flowers for Children*. Each contained dozens of short sketches, poems, stories and playlets, half rewritten from her old *Juvenile Miscellany,* and the rest new.

One of her pieces which became a favorite for many generations to come—it is still found in school readers— was "The New England Boy's Song About Thanksgiving Day." The first verse ran:

> *Over the river, and through the wood,*
> *To Grandfather's house we go;*
> *The horse knows the way,*
> *To carry the sleigh,*
> *Through the white and drifted snow.*

The first volume was affectionately dedicated to John Hopper, her young friend, who was soon to marry Rosa DeWolf, the pretty daughter of a Rhode Island slave trader. Rosa's marriage into an abolitionist family was violently opposed by her father, but Maria, taking great pleasure in the Montague-Capulet romance, helped the couple to plot an elopement.

Only a year after he took over editorship of the *Standard,* David too resigned, in protest against Garrison's disuniting policy and his refusal to support political action.

This made it all the more necessary for Maria to earn money by her writing. For the next few years David was away from home a good part of the time, usually in

Washington to lobby for abolition measures. Maria admired what he was doing, knew it was necessary although miserably paid, if paid at all. She saw what good effect it had in bolstering the small antislavery forces in Congress. But of course she missed him badly. "And just as we were getting comfortably and cozily settled," she lamented to Ellis Loring. "I hate politics worse and worse!"

To her first book of *Letters from New York* she had now added a second. It proved as popular as the first, both running into ten editions or more. She also gathered several of her sketches of "the sins of the city," published in many periodicals, and put them into a book called *Fact and Fiction*. It was a plea for woman's rights; most of the stories showed the wrongs suffered by women in a society whose laws were written by men in their own favor.

In 1847, with David away on an engineering project in Tennessee, Maria spent the summer in New Rochelle, a village thirty miles north of New York. She stayed in the home of Joseph Carpenter, a Quaker abolitionist who had made his house a station on the Underground Railroad.

After her years in New York, this was living in a perfectly dead calm, out of the way of all excitement and all news. But rural life soothed and refreshed her. She wrote little in those months, comforting herself with the wisdom of an old Quaker's remark: "It is a nice thing to say nothing, when thou hast nothing to say."

Now and then she would trudge the four miles to the

depot to catch a train for New York. She was always sure of a welcome at the Hoppers', and a bed. She heard music, saw art shows, and went to a few small parties. One night she went to see a great moving panorama showing scenes from twelve hundred miles of the Mississippi. It was painted on three miles of canvas, attached to rollers which exposed one scene after another as a stagehand turned them from behind a proscenium.

The unending canvas had glaring defects, Maria thought, "but it really seemed as if the sluggish river rolled before us, unfolding a series of rocky bluffs, houses, cotton fields, sugar plantations, steamboats, rafts, and snags with alligators in ambush."

The painter—probably the New Yorker John Banvard —stood on the side and told his adventures out West as the panorama reeled by. He pointed out a type of boat constructed to move in very shallow water, and said the captain of one of them advertised that "it would slip across the country anywhere, after a heavy dew."

Despite such entertainments, Maria couldn't wait to quit the city. "The more I am brought in contact with the world, the more I long for solitude. True wisdom consists in being satisfied with the pleasures we can derive from the common and simple things of life."

Before January had passed she was back in her quiet den at New Rochelle. "I have not heard a dog bark since I have been here," she wrote a Salem friend, "and am of course completely out of the wake of lions. In the stillness of twilight the whizz of the very far-off steam-cars sometimes reaches my ears, and that is all I hear of the turmoil of the world. I eat well, sleep well, dream pleasantly, think very kindly of all mankind, and my days pass away in peace and contentment."

Invited by Massachusetts friends to visit in Salem, or drive up to Lenox, she refused: "You cannot imagine how I hate to go from home. Life flows very sluggishly with me. My aspirations have all come down to a warm blanket, a cup of tea, and a quiet corner to die in."

But that mood came and went. The same letters reveal she went into New York quite often, sometimes staying a month at a time, studying the new paintings and making comparisons between the latest musical virtuosos imported from Europe. And of course she did her part whenever runaways stole silently in the night to Joseph Carpenter's door. Once, when she was home alone, she opened the door to a soft tapping and found the sad and weather-beaten face of a fugitive peering at her from the ragged folds of an old cloak. They had sold his wife and baby to far Louisiana, he told her, and he would never see them again. He had been hired out at work thirteen days, his wages going into another man's pocket, and when he came home he "found the cabin cold."

Maria fed and warmed him at the fire, gave him better clothing, and then helped him along the route toward

Canada, burning with shame because the man could not be free in his own country.

In the spring of 1849 Maria had to leave the Carpenters. They had bought more farm land and needed her room for the laborers they were hiring. So she went back to Friend Hopper's, renting a small garret room from him.

With her she brought a bundle of notes for a new book. For a year she had been reading diligently and widely to gather information for a history of religion through the ages. She was finding it hard and slow going. This was an ambitious project it would take years, she saw, to complete.

She seemed to have lost any desire to write about the momentous events of her own time. The *People's Journal* in England asked her to contribute a monthly article, and despite the pay they offered she replied she couldn't, because "I seem to have hopelessly lost my interest in the world and all it contains."

Thoughts of death troubled her, too, as she neared the age of fifty. Perhaps living in complete solitude for months at a time, and reading much about God and the soul, made her feel its imminence. In this mood, she read through over three hundred old letters received from friends, and burned them all for fear that they might reveal personal secrets.

Settled into Isaac Hopper's again, she continued research on her history of religion while she made silk scarves which she sold at $1.25 to friends. David returned to New York, this time staying for the winter. "A second honeymoon," Maria said, "mixed with making and mending to get him into repair."

But the "honeymoon" did not last long. Once more they had to make a decision. David had no job to anchor him to New York, and Maria, who could do her writing anywhere, felt it her duty to be nearer to her father. He was living in Wayland now, near Boston, and, at eighty-four, was growing more helpless and eccentric. True, Maria's brother James, a prosperous farmer, lived only half a mile from their father, but apparently he would not take on responsibility for the old man. So Maria and David packed up their few belongings and moved into a house at West Newton rented to them by Ellis Loring.

Maria remembered how bitterly she had wept when she had to come to New York alone. Yet when she was forced to leave the city because David was without home or occupation, she wept just as bitterly to go back to the country and "the old tiresome routine of cooking and sweeping."

They were not far from Wayland. Maria thought this way they could avoid the hardship of living under the same roof with her father, and still be close enough to visit him often. David would farm the land and thus they would get along. But nothing worked out that way. They had no money to hire labor, and at his age David's strength wasn't up to conquering the incredibly rocky soil. No matter how hard they both worked, they could not get enough to pay Mr. Loring any rent. He never asked them for anything, but their pride wouldn't let them live permanently on his generosity. At the end of 1853 they moved to Wayland, once again sharing a home with Maria's father.

These were dreary years for Maria. "I have done building castles in the air," she wrote Mrs. Shaw. "I do not now construct even the smallest paper ones. My experiment at West Newton taught me many things which I shall have no need to learn over again. All my dreams have settled into a stoical resignation to life, as it comes." Yet still she hoped for more. "When the tree stands leafless in the winter storm, it is laying up sap for next year's growth, and perhaps I also am gaining strength for new growth somewhere . . . ."

Wayland seemed an unlikely place to find that growth. The quiet town of fifteen hundred people was fifteen miles west of Boston. Twice a day down the Old Sudbury Road past their house came the dusty yellow stagecoach carrying mail and a few passengers. It lumbered into town behind its four horses and, going by Maria's door, made the only break in the local monotony. Luckily, Wayland could claim distinction in one respect: its public library. It was the second place in America to establish one; even in Maria's day, there were only sixty-five public libraries in the whole country. She found books there which helped her to prepare her history of religion.

Maria's cottage stood near the Sudbury River, which in the spring overflowed the broad meadows and made her view a wide lake bordered by forest and hills. In the quiet summer white-sleeved men and boys moved over the meadows scything the hay. Maria kept a garden patch terraced into the hill slope where she raised flowers, fruits, and vegetables. Before the door stood two tall trees, a willow and an elm. At the foot of the hill behind her house were two small ponds, full of lilies all summer. In the spring, wild honeysuckle grew around their borders.

The house itself, built around 1815, was small and simple, and its furniture plain and old-fashioned. Maria mounted a few engravings on the walls, and placed her favorite keepsakes on the shelf of her sitting room.

Then she went back to work on her great labor, the history of religion. It had been interrupted for a while, when Isaac Hopper had died. The old man—a living bridge between Ben Franklin's time and Maria's—had been a tireless reformer. The poor, the abused, the imprisoned, the insane, the enslaved—all knew him for their friend. His going was a great loss to Maria, who had found a warm shelter in his home for so many years. She set about at once to write his biography. *Isaac T. Hopper: a True Life,* published in 1853, suffered from haste, but it captured his humanity in the many anecdotes it recorded from his long and rich life of service. Partly, too, the book was a defense of this radical Quaker from the attacks often made upon him by the conservative friends who opposed his abolitionism.

The book was popular, selling twelve thousand copies quickly, and it was to remain in print until after Maria's own death.

As often happens to writers, Maria's next book, the most arduous effort of her life, had the smallest success. *The Progress of Religious Ideas Through Successive Ages* appeared in three volumes in 1855.

Maria favored no creed. She did not attend any church, she said, "because one offered me petrifactions, and another gas, when I was hungry for bread." She accepted a Divine Being: "The human family are all children of the same Father, though they call Him by different names, and serve Him in different ways."

Because hers was the first American book to look at Christianity objectively, she expected strong criticism and little sympathy. But it brought her a great many letters from readers who expressed their hope that since all faiths sought the same end, a universal church might one day embrace everyone. A few religious periodicals were violent against her. But Rev. Samuel J. May commended it from his pulpit as "the most valuable contribution to an enlarged, charitable, and true theology, that has been made by any one in our country." Emerson called it "a noble gift" and Parker "a magnificent book written in the spirit of humanity."

Financially, the book was an utter failure. It sold very

slowly, and did not go into a second edition. She never received a dollar for it. But she had not expected to make money with it. She simply hoped it would do some good in a world increasingly torn by religious and sectarian quarrels.

Not long after the book appeared, Maria had her daguerreotype made. She was fifty-four then—"quite old enough to have one's likeness taken," she said. Then, looking at the result, she added wryly: "It is not worthwhile to picture the human habitation of the soul, when the tenement is in ruins; it don't look so picturesque as old abbeys and amphitheatres, and even *they* look better by the dimness of moonlight."

11 &8 Song for Free Soil Men

From her sleepy corner of Massachusetts, Maria watched it coming. By turns she felt sorrowful and furious as she followed the political maneuvers in Congress. In 1854, when the Nebraska Bill was passed, repealing the Missouri Compromise and throwing the western territory open to slavery, she denounced the Senate for being so servile to the slave interests. The South will blindly rush upon her own destruction, dragging us after her, she predicted.

Then came the Anthony Burns affair, almost next door to her. "Only three days ago," she hotly wrote a friend traveling in Europe, "another poor slave was hunted in

Boston, and though the general indignation was excited, he was given up by Boston magistrates, and triumphantly carried back to bondage, guarded by a strong escort of U.S. troops. The courthouse was nearly *filled* with troops and hired ruffians, armed with cutlasses and bowie knives. No *citizen* was allowed to enter without a pass, as is the custom with *slaves,* and these passes were obtained with great difficulty, none being given to anyone suspected of being friendly to the slave . . . .

"My dear friend, my very soul is sick, in view of these things . . . . Whether there is *any* limit to the servile submission of the North, I know not. The South seems resolved to try to the utmost how much kicking and cuffing she will bear . . . ."

With Kansas opened to settlement under Senator Douglas' "popular sovereignty" formula, proslavery and antislavery settlers rushed into the territory, determined to swing it their way. By the spring of 1856, the plains of Kansas were a bloody battleground. Lawrence was taken and sacked by the Border Ruffians and in retaliation John Brown and his men killed five proslavery colonists at Pottawatomie Creek. In the Senate, Charles Sumner of Massachusetts, Maria's idolized friend, rose to deliver a powerful assault upon the South for "The Crime Against Kansas," and in retaliation was beaten into bloody unconsciousness by a South Carolina congressman.

News of the outrage upon Sumner sickened Maria. If I could only do something, she thought. She was never one who knew how to serve the Lord by standing and waiting—and to stand and wait now! It almost drove her mad. But the wave of revulsion that swept the North over the attack on Sumner made her more hopeful. Such a man "will not bleed and suffer in vain," she wrote. "Those noble martyrs of liberty in Kansas will prove visionary ghosts, walking through the land, rousing the nation from its guilty slumbers."

In a few weeks the political conventions met to nominate presidential candidates. The new Republican Party chose the explorer, Colonel John C. Fremont. He stood for the admission of Kansas as a free state, with the right of Congress to control slavery in the territories. "I would almost lay down my life to have him elected," Maria said. "There never has been such a crisis since we were a nation. If the slave-power is checked now, it will never regain its strength. If it is not checked, civil war is inevitable; and with all my horror of bloodshed, I could be better resigned to that great calamity than to endure the tyranny that has so long trampled on us."

Maria did not stand around waiting to see how Fremont would do. She pitched into two campaigns at once: to aid the antislavery colonists in Kansas and to elect Fremont. She begged merchant friends for cheap calico and unbleached factory cotton, and organized the wives and daughters of Wayland into sewing parties. Cold weather was coming on in Kansas, and the emigrants—great numbers of them from New England—would be down with fever and ague if warm clothing wasn't hurried to them before the baggage wagons bogged down. Day and night she worked, sitting up by herself till eleven, stitching up sixty yards of cloth as fast as her fingers could go. She scrimped and scraped and saved every penny she could, cleaning the house from roof to cellar herself to put into the Kansas fund what it would have cost to hire help for the house work.

Overnight she turned into a propaganda mill, pouring out personal letters to friends and public letters to the press, urging everyone to get out and work for Fremont. She herself had never placed much faith in political elections, and she confessed to friends that she still did not. "During several of the last elections," she wrote Sarah Shaw, "I have been so much in the way of knowing of the artifices used, and the frauds practiced, especially at the *close* of the campaign, that I have had little hope honesty and freedom would carry the day. The fact is, we have long been governed by a Southern aristocracy. The people *think* they elect their rulers, but they do not. Their rulers are elected by puppets, whose wires are in Southern hands."

When Americans praised themselves for their superiority, her disgust was so open that she was sometimes called unpatriotic. She brought the Boston *Post* down hard upon her for a campaign verse she published about President Pierce. "I couldn't *help* it," she replied. "His name wouldn't rhyme to anything but *curse.*"

Taking again to her pen, she wrote a "Song for the Free Soil Men" which was scattered broadside about the country. All that summer she worked at furious speed on a short novel called *The Kansas Emigrants*. Finished in the early autumn, she sent it to Horace Greeley. He decided to run it in the New York *Tribune* as a serial, interrupting Dickens' *Little Dorrit* to make room for Maria.

David, meanwhile, had gone to work for the Kansas Aid Committee, traveling through the Northeast. So Maria had to make shirts for him and repair his winter clothing while she stood off the printers clamoring for her copy.

As voting day drew close, she tried to make sure that everyone would be on hand at the polls. "If you *don't* come," she warned David, "I shall put on your old hat and coat and vote *for* you."

To Sarah Shaw, she lamented, "What a shame that women can't vote! We'd carry our 'Jessie' [Mrs. Fremont] into the White House on our shoulders, wouldn't we? Never mind! Wait a while! Woman stock is rising in the market. I shall not live to see women vote, but I'll come and rap on the ballot-box. Won't you? I never was bitten by politics before, but such mighty issues are depending on this election that I cannot be indifferent."

Feeble as Maria's ninety-year-old father had become, he insisted on going out to vote that November day. "My *first* vote was given to Washington," said he, "and my *last* shall be given to Fremont." They had to carry him to the polls, and when the news came that his candidate had lost, he wept. Buchanan, the South's choice, would be President. But Fremont had come in second, and the old Whig Party, a poor third, was giving way to the rising Republicans.

Maria's father was near his end. For months she had been at his side day and night, lifting him up and putting him down, feeding him with a spoon, trying to catch the rambling words from a broken mind. As she awaited the old man's death—with David away—her life in those last weeks was as lonely and desolate as solitary imprisonment. Watching her father go, just as the year went out, Maria felt there was nothing so sad on earth as the decay of old age, with a man's spirit so subordinated to his body. She could not settle down again to work. She went into Boston for a few days to seek comfort from friends, but the dreariness went with her. And when she came home, the house all dark and silent, she almost cried herself blind.

12 ☍ Fires Underground

The year that followed her father's death was a quiet one for Maria. She found it hard to settle down to any-thing, although she knew work would be the only cure for her bleakness. One day seemed so much like another that the baker's semiweekly calls were the only things that enabled her to give the days a name. There were the meals to prepare, and cleaning up, and writing letters, and tending the garden, and the everlasting job of mend-ing by the window in the evening, while the stars watched through the leaves of the tall old elm. If the stage stopped before her door, it was an exciting event. It might bring her nephew from Boston to liven a few days with his young view of the world, or books and other gifts from thoughtful friends. The Shaws, leaving for a trip abroad, sent her $100 in gold, "in case of an emergency," they said. Maria promptly gave $20 to a young friend in even poorer circumstances, used $15 for her own pleasure —chiefly to hear music—and put the remainder away "for future dissipation." That meant, as a letter revealed, "not to do anything *useful* with it except to give it away, which is to me the greatest of *all* luxuries."

The Benzons, wealthy friends now living in Europe, invited Maria to be their guest abroad for three years. Maria was dazzled by the magnificent offer, for she had traveled so little. "It seems a shame to go out of this world without seeing any more of it than the head of a pin," she said. But the invitation did not include David, and she would not leave him.

Still without money, and never to have any, Maria constantly wrestled with the problem of prosperous friends who tried however tactfully to help her and David. It took her a long time to call Mr. Shaw "Frank," and when she did, he laughed and said, "At last, Maria, you have forgiven me for being a rich man's son!"

With one such friend, Mrs. Marianna Silsbee of Salem, she had an additional problem. Mr. Silsbee had been the mayor of Salem and was treasurer of Harvard University. Maria's views on politics and slavery were at odds with those of this wealthy ship-owning family. Mrs. Silsbee yearned for her husband to go to Congress and thought he would have made it if it were not for the abolitionists and their influence. The two women saw each other whenever possible, and developed a warm correspondence that lasted many years. But it was hard to throw a plank bridge over the chasm that separated their deep beliefs. During the uproar over the return of Anthony Burns to slavery, Mrs. Silsbee called it "making a ridiculous fuss about one nigger." Maria left her home in a rage. Later, she was calm enough to answer a letter from Mrs. Silsbee. You don't understand the barrier between us, Maria wrote, or even why there need be a barrier because you have never realized the depth and strength of my feelings. You are "simply amused" by the zeal of the reformer, while I have staked social and literary success on the issue of these questions, and hold myself ready to stake my life.

Then she tried to make Mrs. Silsbee see why the issue was so crucial: "I feel keenly and deeply on the subject of slavery, not merely from motives of justice and humanity toward the colored race, but because I see so clearly that *all* the fair prospects of this broad and beautiful land have for years been driving toward an inevitable wreck on that rock so carefully concealed beneath a smooth surface."

Maria's letters now are full of her comments on the writers of her day. When Elizabeth Barrett Browning's long poem, *Aurora Leigh,* appeared, she found it full of strength and beauty, and relished the strong way it struck at the artificial distinctions of society. "A Milton among women!" she exclaimed. "How glad I am that genius is under the necessity of being ever on the free and progressive side! How I delight in having old fogies tormented, always and everywhere!"

She was astonished to find so many interesting novels coming out. Any one of them, she said, would have made a glorious reputation for a writer in earlier years. "It is a trying time for us authors," she said; "the market is so glutted with superior specimens in our commodities. I am so overwhelmed with this conviction that I feel no heart to touch pen to paper again. *Aurora Leigh,* especially, withered me all up with its scorching superiority."

It was a dry season for Maria. For a few years the only work of hers to appear was a collection of her tales and sketches, including the serialized Kansas novel. The title she gave her book—*Autumnal Leaves*—sounded as though she thought her career was coming to an end.

But events and people soon drew her back into action. She went into Boston to help at the Anti-Slavery Fair, and while there, Senator Sumner called upon her and spent a few hours in quiet talk. She saw Senator Henry Wilson, too, and heard his stories of how tense and dangerous the atmosphere in the capital was. She went to the theater, hearing Fanny Kemble give readings from Shakespeare, and seeing a new play called *Farmer Jackwood* which showed slave-catchers outwitted by Vermont farmers.

A few days later the Massachusetts Anti-Slavery Society held its twenty-fifth anniversary meeting, but many of the founders were missing. Maria and David stood by in silent disagreement with Garrison's disunion policy. Now—since Kansas—they were all for political action. Yet mixed with it was a feeling of despair. The ship was sinking. "The United States is not a beacon," Maria cried out, "not a light of freedom! She is a *warning,* rather than an *example* to the world!"

Two months later, Chief Justice Taney handed down his decision on Dred Scott, proclaiming that Negroes were pieces of property with no rights that the white man had to respect anywhere. While the South rejoiced, great mass meetings in the North protested furiously. The sweeping decision, if enforced, could spread slavery throughout the nation.

But in the way the Supreme Court divided Maria could see a glimmer of hope that times might be changing. One of the two justices who dissented from Taney was Curtis of Massachusetts, the very man who had been attorney for the slave owner in the Med case. Now here he was on the Supreme Court bench on the other side, arguing *against* slavery!

Out of Illinois came another sign. Aiming for a seat in the Senate, Abraham Lincoln was saying, "A house divided against itself cannot stand. I believe this government cannot endure permanently half slave and half free. I do not expect the Union to be dissolved; I do not expect the house to fall; but I do expect it will cease to be divided. It will become all one thing, or all the other."

That idea, those words even, were not new. Theodore Parker had voiced them before. But now others, far from radical, were taking them up, too, and carrying them to far wider audiences. True, Lincoln lost that campaign, but the results of the 1858 elections showed Maria that the Republican Party was rapidly gaining strength.

From the South itself rose another voice against slavery. Young Hinton Helper of North Carolina had written a passionate book called *The Impending Crisis.* He hated slavery—not because of what it had done to the Negro, for he was full of race prejudice—but because it had ground down and degraded his own people, the millions of poor whites. Slavery was the curse of the South, he cried from the top of a mountain of statistics he had piled up to prove it.

His appeal to the poor whites to unite against the slave-holders could not rouse deadened minds, even where it slipped through rigid walls of censorship. But in the North his hot arguments became a political weapon for the antislavery forces who circulated his book in millions of copies.

Some Republican politicians, attacked by Southerners, hastily backed away from the book, to Maria's disgust. "I have an unmeasured contempt for those who assure the South that they have never read Helper's book. More shame on them! They have no business in Congress unless they had gained the information it imparts; and especially when the South tries to make it a political crime to read and circulate the book, they ought to hasten with all speed to read and lend it. The miserable, selfish cowards!"

Now the whole country smoked with fires burning underground. As the South's newspapers damned Helper for a traitor and a revolutionary its leaders took more aggressive steps to strengthen slavery. The slave traders were now openly running their cargoes into ports, publicly flouting the law, while demands were being made in Congress to legalize the traffic again.

Lincoln's prediction was working out. "Either the opponents of slavery will arrest the further spread of it," he had said, "or its advocates will push it forward."

While politicans and judges argued hotly in court and Congress, one man was deep in the work he believed God had commissioned him to do. His task it was to set the slaves free. Kansas was his training ground. There, with his five sons, he had fought his first skirmishes against slavery. Now, after years of planning, he was ready to attack the slave power in its own stronghold. On October 16, 1859, with his band of sixteen whites and five Negroes, John Brown invaded the South.

13 ☍ Whirlwind at Harpers Ferry

The first news dispatches crackled across the country's front pages. FEARFUL AND EXCITING INTELLIGENCE! NEGRO INSURRECTION AT HARPERS FERRY! EXTENSIVE NEGRO CONSPIRACY IN VIRGINIA AND MARYLAND! SEIZURE OF THE UNITED STATES ARSENAL BY THE INSURRECTIONISTS! SEVERAL PERSONS KILLED! TROOPS DESPATCHED AGAINST THE INSURGENTS!

North and South the words thrilled along every nerve. Was it a widespread plot? Would the slaves rise everywhere? Swiftly the news changed. It was a handful of men, led by John Brown of Kansas fame. In two days he was taken prisoner by government troops. Now the old man, lying wounded on the floor, was being questioned by reporters and by Governor Wise and Senator Mason of Virginia. "Upon what principle do you justify your acts?" they asked him. Calmly he spoke, his words taken down by the New York *Herald:*

"Upon the golden rule, I pity the poor in bondage that have none to help them; that is why I am here; not to gratify any personal animosity, revenge, or vindictive spirit. It is my sympathy with the oppressed and wronged, that are as good as you and as precious in the sight of God . . . . You all have a heavy responsibility, and it behooves you to prepare more than it does me . . . . You may dispose of me easily, but this question is still to be settled—this Negro question—the end of that is not yet."

A little later, awaiting trial in his prison cell, Brown wrote a friend, "I do not feel conscious of guilt in taking up arms; and had it been in behalf of the rich and the powerful, the intelligent, the great—as men count greatness—of those who form enactments to suit themselves and corrupt others, or some of their friends, that I interfered, suffered, sacrificed, and fell, it would have been doing very well."

With Brown lodged in the Charleston jail, letters came to light showing several well-known abolitionists and Republicans in the North had given money and even arms to the old man. At once the proslavery press violently attacked the rising Republican Party for sharing guilt

with John Brown. The Republican newspapers themselves at first tried to discredit Brown as a madman the
party could have no responsibility for.

The South was horrified and enraged by Brown's deed,
but it could not help admiring the old man for his courage and bearing. This old man—was he a hero? Or was
he crazy? Was he alone, or the spearhead of a giant conspiracy? Virginia's Governor Wise himself said, "Brown
is a bundle of the best nerves I ever saw, cut and thrust,
bleeding and in bonds. He is a man of clear head, of
courage, fortitude. He is a fanatic, vain and garrulous, but
firm and truthful and intelligent."

The raid gave a new direction to events. The Union's
political power had been—still was—in the slave owners'
hands. But here came old John Brown, invading their
land and striking slavery at its roots. By its resistance—
often armed—to the Fugitive Slave Law, the North had
shown it was no longer content merely to moralize against
slavery. Was it now ready to risk its skin to crush it?
How many other John Browns were arming themselves
to follow his example?

And when men like Ralph Waldo Emerson spoke up
and called John Brown a "new saint who will make the
gallows glorious like the cross" it was a sign to the South
that behind the man they called a fanatic was a vast public spirit that approved what he had done. To Maria the
raid on Harpers Ferry seemed a mad attempt. "According
to *my* views such violent attempts to right wrong are both

injudicious and evil," she wrote Sarah Shaw. "But Captain Brown takes the *Old* Testament view of things. He is a real psalm-singing, praying Puritan, of the old stamp. Of course, it is simple justice to judge him from his own conscientious point of view. If we praise Concord Fight, where men fought for their own rights, how can we consistently blame this far more disinterested effort for the freedom of others? Deeply as I regret the whole affair, I cannot help honoring the brave old man."

She did not realize how inconsistent she was. A few years earlier she had been hotly in favor of Bostonians storming the courthouse to free a fugitive slave. And had she not backed the antislavery settlers who went rifle in hand to Kansas? Now she was calling John Brown's use of force wrong in one sentence, while finding words to praise him in the next.

As soon as she read that Brown was wounded and a prisoner among enemies, Maria wrote him a letter, offering to come and nurse him in prison. She enclosed this letter in another to Governor Wise, asking his permission to nurse the prisoner. She made clear that she was an uncompromising abolitionist, but was greatly surprised by news of the raid. She pledged not to advance her antislavery opinions in Virginia if the governor would generously permit her to come.

Then Maria waited in suspense with her bundle of linen rags ready for lint. Several days later came the reply, civil but cold: Governor Wise said he would not and could not prevent her coming, but it was up to the local authorities to permit her access to the prisoner. He would offer her the official protection that the United States Constitution guaranteed every citizen. But he warned that with the community so excited by Brown's "crimes," it might be imprudent for her to come and show her sympathy. Then he went on to reprove her. How she could have been "surprised" by the attack on Harpers Ferry he could not understand. Brown's raid, after all, "was a natural consequence of your sympathy, and the errors of that sympathy ought to make you doubt its virtue from the effect on his conduct."

Meanwhile Captain Brown, recovering from his wounds, wrote Maria declining her offer, but asking her instead to help raise funds to aid his wife and three young daughters, and the families of the men who had fallen beside him.

Maria at once set about doing as John Brown had asked. She also thought it worthwhile to reply to Governor Wise's reproof. She meant this to be a private affair, but the New York *Tribune* got hold of the letters in Virginia somehow, and blazoned the exchange in its columns.

Her answer to Wise argued powerfully that it was not the abolitionists who had produced the outbreak but the high-handed encroachments of the slave owners. "They sowed the wind in Kansas," she said, "and have reaped the whirlwind at Harpers Ferry."

If, as John Brown himself declared, he merely intended to free the oppressed, she continued, where could he read a more forcible lesson than is furnished by the state seal of Virginia? A liberty-loving hero stands with his foot upon a prostrate tyrant; under his strong arm, manacles and chains lie broken; and the motto is: *"Sic Semper Tyrannis"—"Thus be it ever done to tyrants."*

"And this," Maria shot home, "is the blazon of a state whose most profitable business is the internal slave-trade! —in whose highways coffles of human chattels, chained and manacled, are frequently seen! And the seal and the coffles are both looked upon by other chattels, constantly exposed to the same fate! What if some Vesey, or Nat Turner, should be growing up among those apparently quiet spectators!"

When the exchange between Maria and Governor Wise reached the public through the *Tribune,* another Virginian joined the discussion. From Mrs. Margaretta Mason, the wife of the Senator, came a scorching letter to Maria which opened:

"Do you read your Bible, Mrs. Child? If you do, read there, 'Woe unto you hypocrites.' "

How dare *you,* Mrs. Mason went on, soothe with sisterly care the old murderer of Harpers Ferry! "When you can equal in deeds of love and charity to those *around* you, what is shown by nine-tenths of the Virginian plantations, then by your 'sympathy' whet the knives for our throats, and kindle the torch that fires our homes."

And at the end, Mrs. Mason added: "No Southerner ought . . . to read a line of your composition, or to touch a magazine which bears your name in its lists of contributors; and in this we hope for the 'sympathy' at least of those at the North who deserve the name of woman."

Maria was not surprised by Mrs. Mason's rage, for by now her postbox had been overwhelmed by abusive letters from the South, as well as by praise from people in the free states. She sat down to compose a reply to Mrs. Mason. Her first impulse was to confess her sympathy for Mrs. Mason's terror, and her horror at the consequences that might have followed from John Brown's attempt. She felt especially compassionate toward the women of the South. If they could only see that their insecurity grew out of the hateful institution they cherished so blindly!

But then Maria reasoned that Mrs. Mason would take such sympathy, from an abolitionist, as sheer hypocrisy. Besides, as she explained to Sarah Shaw, "I *force* myself to remember that, terrible as an insurrection would be to *white* women and children, the *black* women and children have, for many generations, been living in subjection to things *as* horrible, with no Union, no laws, no public sentiment to help *them*."

How could anyone be silent in the face of these wrongs, she wondered. To keep quiet when you see crimes committed is really to be an accomplice. No, she knew what she had to do, no matter what the consequences.

So she answered Mrs. Mason, saying she had no desire

to see her hurt, but only wished her well, both in this world and the next. As for John Brown, she would not debate his case, for his body was in charge of the courts and his reputation sure to be in charge of posterity.

I don't care about changing your opinion of me, she said, but I do wish you could be persuaded to examine this subject of slavery dispassionately, for the sake of Virginia's own prosperity and the welfare of unborn generations both white and colored. Yet in the thirty years abolitionists have been trying to reason with slaveholders through the press, and in the halls of Congress, their efforts have been met with violence and abuse almost equal to that poured on the head of John Brown.

"Yet surely we, as a portion of the Union, involved in the expense, the degeneracy, the danger, and the disgrace of this iniquitous and fatal system, have a *right* to speak about it, and a right to be *heard* also."

She pointed out that while the North freely published proslavery arguments, the South would not let its own citizens examine the other side. Mrs. Mason's letter was published in Northern papers as well as Southern, but would Maria's reply be printed in any Southern paper?

"The despotic measure you take to silence investigation, and shut out the light from your own white population," she asserted, "prove how little reliance you have on the strength of your cause. In this enlightened age, all despotisms *ought* to come to an end by the agency of moral and rational means. But if they resist such agencies, it is in the order of Providence that they *must* come to an end by violence. History is full of such lessons."

As for Mrs. Mason's threat that no Southerner ought henceforth to read a line of Maria's writing, that was laughable now. You stopped reading me twenty-seven years ago, after my *Appeal* was published!

Besides, she said, even if I cared about being shut out of the South, I'd have the comfort of being exiled in very good company: Emerson, Whittier, Longfellow, Lowell, Bryant, Harriet Beecher Stowe—they've all sounded the trumpet for moral warfare with slavery—and that's treason by your standards.

"The fact is," she concluded, "the whole civilized world proclaims slavery an outlaw, and the best intellect of the age is active in hunting it down."

December 2 was the day the Virginia court appointed for the hanging of John Brown. The Negro people of Boston held a prayer meeting, and Maria went into the city to spend that solemn day with them. No one there, she found, questioned the old hero's claims to reverence, or doubted the sanity of his mind. "All they knew about it was, that he was the friend of their oppressed race, and that he proved it by dying for them."

They sang hymns, and in between got up to talk about old Brown. One old man informed the Lord that he "had been a slave, and knew how bitter it was." And then he added with great fervor, "since it has pleased thee to take away our Moses, oh! Lord God! raise us up a Joshua!" To which all the congregation responded with a loud "Amen!"

As John Brown was taken from jail on that morning of his execution, he left with the guard a piece of paper on which he had scrawled: "I John Brown am now quite certain that the crimes of this guilty land will never be purged away but with blood. I had, as I now think, vainly flattered myself that without very much bloodshed it might be done."

Around the scaffold, under Colonel Robert E. Lee's command, were massed two thousand troops. "This is a beautiful country," Brown said as the death wagon drew up and his eyes lifted to the Blue Ridge Mountains. He climbed the gallows steps quickly. The white hood dropped over his head and the rope—made of cotton, by slave labor—was placed around his neck. A blow of the sheriff's hatchet, and the body dropped through the trap door. Thirteen minutes later, the physician pronounced him dead.

In less than two years, an army of two million was marching south to crush slavery, singing "John Brown's body lies a-moldering in the grave, but his soul goes marching on."

14&&& "From This Time Till I Die"

As soon as Maria had drafted her reply to Mrs. Mason's letter, she sent it to Horace Greeley, urging him to print the correspondence in his *Tribune*. Publication would help the Republican Party, she said. The facts would give people entering wedges for their arguments. "Many don't know the facts; others need to be reminded of them."

So powerful was the effect in the press that the American Anti-Slavery Society decided to issue her correspondence with the Virginians as a pamphlet. Over 300,000 copies were sold, an enormous circulation for that day, greater than for anything else she had written.

John Brown's martyrdom gave her new life. "Before

this affair," she said, "I thought I was growing old and drowsy, but now I am as strong as an eagle."

She thought of a dozen ways to promote the circulation of her pamphlet and widen its impact. She had copies sent abroad to Harriet Martineau, to Kossuth, Victor Hugo, Mazzini. She wrote to Queen Victoria about John Brown.

To London newspapers and magazines she sent letters explaining the causes of John Brown's act. "The fact is," she said, "I want to shoot the accursed institution from all quarters of the globe. I think, from this time till I die, I shall stop firing only long enough to load my guns."

Now she felt she was sharing some of John Brown's own faith in "fore-ordination." The Lord, she believed, had put it into her heart to write that letter to Brown in jail, so that she might be whirled aloft by the excitement and so command a larger audience.

In later years, looking back at the abolition struggle, she thought these letters were her most notable achievement. They had been one among the innumerable elements that had helped prepare the North for the final conflict.

In March, as the last two of Brown's men to be tried were being readied for execution, Maria went from door to door in Wayland and secured three hundred signatures to a petition for mercy. But no effort could help them, and they too died on the scaffold. Letters continued to pour in on her, praising or denouncing her stand on

Brown. In one week, she answered forty-three. "It gives me a grand chance to do mischief," she said, "and I do it with all diligence."

With the nation's ear now waiting for anything she had to say, she followed up swiftly. Three more antislavery pamphlets appeared in the next months: *The Duty of Disobedience to the Fugitive Slave Act; The Patriarchal Institution;* and *The Right Way, the Safe Way, Proved by Emancipation in the West Indies and Elsewhere.*

She prepared the first—an open message to the Massachusetts legislature—in a state of great excitement. To her amazement, she felt more indignant than in her younger days. "I *ought* to grow calmer," she confessed, "but I do not!"

Again she pitched in to help distribute her pamphlets. Somehow she got lists of hundreds of Virginians, and mailed the tracts south to over twelve hundred people, addressing the envelopes and paying the postage herself. She also got the names of Southern students attending Northern colleges, hoping to win them over by fact and reason. "It shall not be *my* fault," she said, "if the wicked system is not abolished by wiser and better means than bloodshed." But only one Southerner replied to her.

Nevertheless, her energy, renewed and flooding, drove her on to task after task. Garrison asked her to take on the editing of the antislavery almanac. She didn't like that kind of cut-and-paste-and-patch job, and at first she refused. Then, her conscience troubling her, she confessed she felt mean to have said no. She had no right to refuse any kind of work that she could do for human freedom. How could she shirk drudgery when the slave toiled incessantly and hopelessly?

Shortly, when Garrison fell ill, she wrote to urge him to rest and recover. She and David would help edit the *Liberator* in his absence, or take care of the office. And she went on to offer him medical advice: "Don't sit in *overstuffed* chairs. I believe the back is much weakened by the warmth of modern furniture."

It was about this time that Maria saw a letter from Thomas Sims, the fugitive slave who in 1851 had been shipped back to bondage from Boston. Sims had now written from Georgia to his sister in Boston, expressing an intense longing for his freedom. Because he was a skillful mechanic, his master was asking $1,800 for him. Maria swore that as Massachusetts had sent him into slavery, Massachusetts should bring him back. And with *proslavery money*. It would be impossible for an abolitionist to get that big a sum out of proslavery purses, her friends all said. But she would do it, even if it meant writing a hundred letters, or stationing herself on the State House steps to besiege people.

Her luck seemed to hold. She had written only eighteen letters when back came an answer from one man saying he would pay the whole sum if she would not mention his name. It was Charles Devens. As a United States marshal, he had felt obliged to carry out the Fugitive Slave Law and had helped send Sims back to his master in Savannah. But it had so pained his heart at the time, and troubled his conscience ever since, that he was eager to try to atone for his error. The plan fell through, however, and Sims had to wait for his freedom until the Civil War liberated him. Then, when the ex-slave found his way North again, Devens, now a major general in the Union army, sent him $100 through Maria and helped him find a government job.

In May the Republicans met in Chicago and nominated Lincoln for President on a platform that aimed at winning support from conservatives and radicals alike. The party was against the extension of slavery, but would not interfere with the right of each state to control its own affairs.

Maria gave her support to Lincoln, but not enthusiastically. For her the Republican Party's only value to the cause of freedom was that it couldn't avoid keeping alive discussion of the issue of slavery.

"As for Lincoln himself," she said, "I believe his nature is honest and true, but he is in the hands of politicians."

Running against three candidates, Lincoln won a majority of the electoral votes, but only 40 per cent of the popular vote. As he sat at home in Springfield, waiting to take office, seven states of the deep South seceded, took over federal forts and arsenals, and called a convention to write their own constitution.

In Washington, President Buchanan told Congress that

in his opinion the federal government had no power to stop secession. Most Americans, North and South, dreaded war and hoped some compromise could be found to keep the peace. Maria—like many of the abolitionists —didn't regret seeing the slave states leave. She only wished the border states would go out too, and leave the North wholly free.

Compromise designed to conciliate slaveholders and keep them in the Union was wrong, the abolitionists felt. "Let the erring sisters go in peace," they said. They wanted no Civil War. Business interests too found a bond with abolitionists on this point. If war came, the $200,-000,000 the South owed Northerners would be lost.

In Congress, politicians maneuvered feverishly to conciliate the South, offering great concessions on slavery if only the secessionists would return. Disgusted by the spectacle of "selfishness, servility and cowardice," Maria thought only Charles Sumner and a handful of others were keeping their balance in the desperately rocking boat.

In Boston, mobs attacked abolitionist meetings in the hope of silencing men like Wendell Phillips who were ready to shovel slave states out of the Union. Three times the orator spoke within a few weeks and each time bloodthirsty rioters were held off only by police squads or the abolitionist's armed friends.

The dreadful revival of mobs—no one had forgotten the year 1835—moved to a climax in Boston. Phillips was to speak at the annual meeting of the Massachusetts Anti-Slavery Society at Tremont Temple on January 24. He did not move on the streets without his hand on his revolver. Police protection was asked for the abolitionist convention, but the new Democratic mayor refused it. On the eve of the meeting, Maria went to a reception at Mrs. Chapman's. Banners and music and old friends almost made Maria forget what tomorrow threatened. Wearied by the long hours, she walked to her lodgings through streets silvered in moonlight and icicles. She knew secret preparations were being made to mob the antislavery meeting the next day, and that the mayor was openly on the side of the mob. Excited and anxious for Wendell Phillips' safety, she could not sleep. Hour after hour she heard the clock strike while visions of Phillips bloodied under murderous blows passed through her mind.

Very early the next morning she entered the hall lined with files of young men who had made themselves Phillips' bodyguard. Under their coats all wore arms they were pledged not to use unless any of the speakers was in personal danger. But no one could foresee what might happen.

As the meeting opened, the platform, an eyewitness reported, "was crowded with the faithful and the true—many a tried soldier in Freedom's long battle"—Francis Jackson, Edmund Quincy, James Freeman Clarke, Ralph Waldo Emerson, Samuel J. May, Thomas Wentworth Higginson, Mrs. Maria Chapman, and "Mrs. Lydia Maria

Child, as full of enthusiasm as she could express by flashing eye, glowing cheek, and waving handkerchief, as she sat by the organ on the highest seat of the platform, making everybody glad by her presence."

Hardly had the meeting opened when the mob came tumbling in by the hundreds. They began yelling from the galleries, screeching, stamping, bellowing. For a full hour Phillips stood before them, trying to be heard whenever the storm lulled a little. But the mob would yell again, and sing and howl, and at last surged toward the platform as Maria's heart beat so fast she could hear it. But the armed abolitionists formed a firm wall which would not give to the mob's battering. When the meeting ended, Phillips used a private exit to avoid the rioters waiting outside for him. Disappointed by his escape, they rushed to his house, but were kept from his door by police and private guards.

At his inaugural on the fourth of March, Lincoln offered an olive branch to the South: he would not interfere with slavery in the states where it existed, and he promised to support enforcement of the Fugitive Slave Law. But, he warned, if the secessionists chose civil war to destroy the government, he would meet force with force.

Five weeks later, Southern guns fired upon Fort Sumter.

15 &&& The Price of Blood

Maria could think of nothing but the war. In the streets she saw universal enthusiasm for the flag. Fathers and sons rallied to Lincoln's call for troops. "It'll be short and easy," they said; "we'll soon put down the rebels." But was that all, Maria wondered, was that why the war was being fought?

In the Boston *Advertiser* she read a long editorial "proving" that slavery had nothing whatsoever to do with this war. It was a war to put down treason, not to meddle with slavery!

In drowsy little Wayland, David went to a meeting to organize aid for the army. When he said something about the duty of the United States toward slaves who might offer to fight on its side, he was almost mobbed. "The war has nothing to do with the damned niggers!" they yelled. "This war's to preserve the union—we don't want to hear a word about the niggers!"

In the papers, Maria read that thirty slaves had made their way to Fort Pickens, through great peril and suffering, strengthened by the faith that President Lincoln was their friend and that his soldiers would protect them. They asked to serve the United States, but they were put in chains and sent back to their masters, who whipped them almost to death.

Maria was sickened by these reports. "When such things happen under the U.S. flag, I cannot and I will not say 'God bless it!' Nay, unless it ceases from this iniquity, I say, deliberately and solemnly, 'May the curse of God rest upon it! May it be trampled in the dust, kicked by rebels, and spit upon by tyrants!' "

But under the surface of events she saw deeper forces at work. Following the fashion of patriotism, vast numbers were rushing into the great wave of events which they could not control. There was a chance, Maria realized, that the wave would wash out slavery before it subsided. While thousands were joining up merely to make business safe and themselves popular, God would use them for something better than they intended.

She found herself hoping the slaveholders would stick at their rebellion till the emancipation of their slaves was accomplished. Jeff Davis would have to goad the free states into doing, from politics and revenge, what they didn't have the manhood to do from justice and humanity.

No class, she said, except the old abolitionists, seem to take the slaves at all into account. They are property, to be disposed of in any way, according as the laws of war, or the patching up of the Union, may seem to render expedient.

Day by day she followed the progress of the war. Every report of fugitive slaves sent back cut into her heart like the stab of a bowie knife. It wasn't only that she pitied the poor runaway who trusted the government in vain, but because she felt all moral dignity was taken out of the war by such incidents, and that the fervor of the soldiers and the people must be diminished by it.

A soldier needs a great idea to fight for, she said; how can the idea of freedom be upheld this way? And how absurd, how insane it seemed to send back those who want to serve us, to be employed by rebels to help them in shooting us! Were the eyes of government so blind? She began to think defeats were needed to make the Union come up manfully to the work of freedom.

But already there were signs of awakening. "My faith is founded upon the fact that God has so wonderfully ordered events that it is plainly for a purpose," she wrote a friend. Men who a few months ago were the most proslavery demagogues were now talking real fanatical abolitionism. The risk was educating men to higher views of justice and humanity. She heard Professor Ticknor had given $500 to carry on the war. Did it mean even that old aristocrat knew the war was on account of slavery, and nothing else?

She wrote her old friend Whittier, prodding him to use his pen in the war. "Nothing on earth has such effect on the popular heart as songs, which the soldiers would take up with enthusiasm. 'Old John Brown Hallelujah!' is performing a wonderful mission now. Where the words came from, nobody knows, and the tune is an exciting, spirit-stirring thing . . . . It warms up soldiers and boys, and the air is full of it, just as France was of the Marseillaise."

She sought Whittier's support—and William Cullen Bryant's, too—in politics as well as poetry. General Fremont, commanding Union forces in the West, issued a proclamation declaring that slaves of Missourians taking up arms against the United States were free. A few days later Lincoln overruled him. Maria knew how to apply pressure in politics. She understood how to muster public opinion. In a letter to Whittier she urged that every friend of freedom should speak out in support of Fremont. "For *his* sake, and for the *slave's* sake, we ought to rally behind him. We ought never to forget that he was the *first* man to utter the word which millions long to hear . . . . Shall we let the government suppose that the public pulse beats languidly, and thus make it more feeble and timid than it is?"

But she was not rash and destructive in what she wanted to do: move cautiously, she advised Whittier. Thank Fremont for his energy and bravery, but don't say anything against the President. Let Fremont know he has public support. And let the government find out he has it.

I *try* to be patient, she confided to Whittier, "but every once in a while I groan out, O Lord! O Lord! How we *do* need a Cromwell!" And then she went on to another proposal:

"If only the soldiers had a song, proclaiming what they went to fight for, and indignantly announcing they did not go to hunt slaves, to send back to their tyrants poor lacerated workmen who for years had been toiling for the rich without wages—if they had such a song to a tune that excited them, how rapidly it would educate them!"

Ballads, too, she added, told in your pictorial, fascinating style, would be a great work at this crisis.

Whittier listened to Maria's plea, and soon she was delighted by his response. He wrote "The Watchers" and the "Song of the Negro Boatman," the first of many war poems. "So you see," she wrote the Quaker poet, "you are at least equal to a major-general in the forces you lead into the field, and your laurels are bloodless."

As the fall of 1861 came on, Maria became concerned

about the condition of the slaves who were fleeing from their masters and flocking into Fortress Monroe near Washington. An article in a missionary magazine said they would suffer for clothing and bedding in the winter unless the charitable gave a helping hand. Instantly she went to work, making her home a relay station for aid to the "contrabands." Hers was the first package to arrive in response to the appeal.

The government was paying wages to the contrabands they employed, but many had no jobs and had to scramble for a living any way they could. "People are so busy giving and working for the soldiers," Maria observed, "that few think of the poor fugitives." She wrote a missionary friend working among them and found that some of the Negro women could cut and make garments and many were good knitters. So she sent cloth and thread, tape, buttons, needles with it. Out of her own meager funds she spent fifteen dollars for flannel and calico and for two weeks worked as hard as she could drive herself, repairing secondhand garments, and making hoods for the women and woolen caps for the men.

From house to house she went again, as she had done in the Kansas days. She picked up used clothing for children, woolen socks, flannel shirts, yarn, blankets, overcoats, picture books and primary school readers. She dug out all the biographies of runaway slaves she could find, restitching many of them, and putting them in good strong bindings.

From old *Liberators* she snipped out illustrations and pasted on book covers pictures of Christ coming to rescue the oppressed, and the happy Emancipation scene of the children with their lambs, doing it all "as nicely," she said, "as if I were doing it for Queen Victoria."

In the winter she began knitting mittens and socks for the army, "but only for the Kansas troops," she explained. "I can trust them, for they have vowed a vow unto the Lord that no fugitive shall ever be surrendered in their camps."

She worked without letup. One week she was making flannels for the hospitals, the next a hood for a poor neighbor. Odd minutes were filled up with raveling lint; every string that she could get hold of, she said, she pulled for her oppressed black brother. She wrote to the *Tribune* about him, to the *Transcript,* to private individuals, to the President, and to members of Congress.

Gradually, she could sense a change in the public feeling. The way in which the Negro's cause was getting argued and listened to in all quarters was heartening to her: "I try to forget Bull Runs and Fredericksburg retreats, and think only of the increasing rapidity of moral progress . . . ."

Human hands were blundering shockingly, she thought. To her, Lincoln was being "narrow-minded, short-sighted, and obstinate." Early in the war she saw the necessity the government was slow to face up to. "I believe that the *only* way to save our free institutions from utter shipwreck is to summon the slaves to our standard, *forthwith.* If this country *is* to be what our Puritan Fathers *intended,* a government of the *people,* slavery *must* be done away. The War Power is the *only* power that can abolish it; and if *that* is not made use of, no other power *will* abolish it."

She feared that a peace might be patched out of compromises that would leave slavery untouched. If all this blood is shed in vain, if all this land's riches are devastated for nothing, the war will leave us far worse than it found us.

For over two years Lincoln had resisted the demands of the radical Republicans for abolition. He was trying to keep the border states loyal to the Union. But now, as the summer of 1862 came on, the pressures upon him became more intense. With every bloody battle more and more people began to see the wisdom of Maria's position.

On New Year's Day, 1863, the President issued the Emancipation Proclamation. Because the regions it covered were those still controlled by the Confederacy, the act did not free a single slave. Maria wrote Sarah Shaw that she was thankful for the proclamation, "but it excited no enthusiasm in my mind. The ugly fact cannot be concealed that it was done reluctantly and stintedly," as a political and military necessity. But though no halo of moral glory surrounded it, she saw it would do a great good nevertheless.

With the doctrine of emancipation proclaimed, many

began to speculate about the slave's future when the war would be over. How would he earn a living? What kind of citizen would he be? people asked. What can we do with the slaves seemed a foolish question to Maria. "Take them away from Mr. Lash and place them with Mr. Cash" was her way of settling what she thought was only an imaginary difficulty.

What can we do with the *master* was a much harder problem to solve, she said. In a few generations, she thought, the experience of living under free institutions would change the moral and intellectual character of the whole Southern people. But what about the transition period? Wouldn't the Southerners be a troublesome and dangerous set to deal with? Talk about *slaves* being unfit to be trusted with legislation. It seemed to her that everything slaveholders had been molded into made them *more* unfit to legislate for free men.

But there were other questions troubling many minds —social equality and intermarriage—was this to be the future of the two races? The horror some people voiced about these prospects made Maria smile. "The argument is so shallow!" she wrote. "The fear is so contradicting of itself!" And she went on to explain why:

"If there *is* an 'instinctive antipathy,' as many assert, surely that antipathy may be trusted to prevent amalgamation. If there is *no* instinctive antipathy, what reason is there for the horror?

"If the colored people are *really* an 'inferior race,' what danger is there of their attaining to an 'equality' with us? If they are *not* inferior, what reason is there for excluding them from equality?"

Maria believed that when the Negro people had had a chance to attain education and decent living standards the prejudice against them, originating in their degraded position as slaves, would pass away. "Our moral and intellectual estimate of a man will be no more affected by the color of his skin than it now is by the color of his hair." But she thought it would take a long time.

Maria had turned sixty now. When a friend sent her birthday greetings, she replied: "From 45 to 55 the flight of each year made me shudder a little, as I do when November cold gives premonition of approaching winter. But I have got bravely over that. I accept my 60 years serenely, feeling that the age has its compensations for lost advantages."

There were long months when her friends heard nothing from Wayland. There were only her two hands to do everything, especially with David ill for weeks at a time. As winter came on she had to make and repair clothing. When the old carpet got ragged beyond even her powers of darning, turning, and piecing, she made a new one. There was seed to be gathered and labeled, plants to be moved, currant wine to be made, barberry and currant jelly to be made for the hospitals, flannels for the Sanitary Commission, apples to be cut and dried. All that and more, in addition to her everyday routine of cooking, washing, cleaning.

Her Boston friends invited her into town for parties, but the weather seemed too formidable to undertake such a long ride. More and more she wished there were some way to dodge the New England winters.

Childless, she and David shared the sorrows of friends whose sons and nephews were dying day after day on the battlefields. Their hearts ached, but they felt helpless. A dense fog seemed to rest over the future; they could only pray and wait.

Now and then the quiet isolation was interrupted by visits from old friends. In June, Sarah and Frank Shaw came to spend a day. Maria and David were proud to show them what they had done with their small house. It had taken a long while and hard labor to make it cozy and tasteful.

The next day, after their noon meal, David went to work in the garden while Maria napped. Suddenly he smelled smoke and, opening the kitchen door, found the whole room ablaze. Maria was awakened by his agonized screams and stumbled through the blistering passage to safety outdoors. Luckily it was Saturday, with all the neighbors home, and they rallied round with garden hoses to help stop the flames before they could destroy everything. The ell burned down, but the main part of their home was left.

For days Maria could not look the disaster in the face calmly. Her first impulse was to flee the place and seek shelter somewhere, anywhere. But then her confidence returned and she and David decided to stay through the summer, gradually cleaning, mending, and salvaging what they could, and then go to Boston to board for the fall and winter. The next spring, they would return and do major repairs.

But the summer was not over. New horrors crowded in.

The heaviest blow fell when the only son of Maria's dear friends, the Shaws, was killed. Young Robert Gould Shaw, married only a few weeks, had volunteered to serve with the Fifty-fourth Massachusetts, one of the first Negro regiments permitted to fight. With hardly any combat training, the Fifty-fourth was sent into action at the storming of Fort Wagner, and Colonel Shaw, at the head of his troops, was killed. He was buried in a mass grave with his Negro soldiers by a Confederate commander who thought somehow this would humiliate the Boston abolitionist even after death.

Maria wrote the grieving mother and father, seeking to comfort them. "How strange it is that every inch of freedom in this world has to be bought at the price of so much blood."

In mid-July New York mobs rioted against the Draft Law and raged through the streets for four days, burning and pillaging homes and lynching Negroes. One of the houses they gutted belonged to James Gibbons, Maria's abolitionist friend who had worked with her on the *Anti-Slavery Standard*. Her own disaster had left her stunned and desolate, but now she reproached herself for having cared so much about a home when so many others were being ruthlessly broken up. The debris of a fire was bad, but what was it compared with the desolation wrought by a lynch mob?

To divert her mind from the perpetual horrors of war, she began collecting poems, stories, and essays about old age. She was thinking of publishing a book on the subject. She wanted every word of her collection to be bright and cheerful. Too many people, when they talked to the old, seemed to think it necessary to bring up decay and death. There was no need of that, since the old naturally had a tendency to think too much upon it.

Ticknor & Fields published *Looking Towards Sunset* in 1864. The first edition sold out within the year. Like all her work, it proved both useful and entertaining. She gave the elderly hints on health and cleanliness (more than thirty years earlier she had given similar advice to the young), told the unmarried how to make themselves useful, and most importantly, urged the old to plunge into the currents of life around them, and not to stand on the shore. Take part in the political and social struggles of the age, she said, and you won't stagnate.

Maria was pleased beyond measure by the response to her book, for the proceeds were pledged to the aid of the freedmen. That she could cheer old folks with one hand, and help the wronged and suffering with the other, was the highest satisfaction. She got a charming note from William Cullen Bryant on the book, and Wendell Phillips wrote that she had given him and his wife much delight.

16 ⛓ The Freedmen's Book

The summer of 1864 began with the country in deep gloom. In one month of campaigning in the Wilderness, Grant lost sixty thousand men—the size of Lee's whole army. The war seemed to be turning into one unbroken funeral procession. There were quarrels in the President's Cabinet, the Copperheads were openly predicting defeat, much of the press was savagely attacking the conduct of the war.

The abolitionists hotly debated whether to support Lincoln for a second term. Wendell Phillips led one faction that thought Lincoln was ready to make a sham peace that would leave the freedmen under the control of the slaveholders. Garrison thought there was more hope for the President than that. Most of the abolitionists felt the way Maria did. "Old Abe," she wrote Whittier, "deserves his reputation for honesty, and I have no doubt he has a hearty abhorrence of slavery, though he lacks sympathy with the colored people. He is a man of details, I think, incapable, by nature and habit, of taking large, comprehensive views. But is it not much to have an *honest* man? Who is there, who would be better?"

So sick of war and tired of blood were the people that men like Greeley thought Lincoln was already defeated. He could not be re-elected; too many thought his candidacy a misfortune. His own party leaders openly insulted him, and a majority of the Republicans in Congress opposed him. Ten weeks before the election Lincoln predicted he would lose. But then Sherman's army marched to the sea, capturing Atlanta, and Northern morale took a sharp upturn.

The nation went to the polls on November 8, a day Maria had looked forward to with much anxiety. "I never before have cared to vote," she said, "but today it makes me sad that I cannot. To think that a drunken Irishman may decide the destiny of this great nation, while I, who have so long and carefully watched all the springs in the machinery of State, would be contemptuously thrust from the polls! What a burlesque on human institutions!"

Lincoln carried by 212 to 21 electoral votes; his popular majority was 400,000 out of 4,000,000 votes. Maria was happy at the result. She felt the American form of government rested on secure foundations. In spite of the general lack of enthusiasm for old Abe, in spite of the many maneuvers by which the politicians had tried to force him out of the race, in spite of the long, long drag upon the people's patience and resources which the war had produced—in spite of all this—he had won.

"I call this the triumph of free schools," Maria said, "for it was the intelligence and reason of the people that re-elected Abraham Lincoln . . . . With all his deficiencies, it must be admitted that he has grown continually; and, considering how slavery had weakened and perverted the moral sense of the whole country, it was great good luck to have the people elect a man who was willing to grow."

Early in 1865, something prompted Maria to set down on paper all the things she had done the year before. Heading the sheets "Employments in 1864," she wrote out this list:

Wrote 235 letters
Wrote 6 articles for newspapers
Wrote 47 autograph articles for newspapers
Wrote my Will
Corrected proofs for Sunset *book*
Read aloud 6 pamphlets and 21 volumes
Read to myself 7 volumes
Made 25 needle books for Freedwomen

2 *Bivouac caps for soldiers*

Knit 2 pair of hospital socks

Gathered and made peck of pickles for hospitals

Knit 4 pair of socks for David

Knit and made up 2 pair of suspenders for D.

Knit 6 baby shirts for friends

Knit 1 large Afghan & made the fringe

Made 1 spectacle case for David

Made 1 door mat

Made 1 lined woollen cape

Made 3 pair of corsets

  2 *shirts for D.*

  1 *chemise*

  2 *flannel shirts for D.*

Cut and made three gowns

1 *shirt with waist*

1 *thick cotton petticoat*

1 *quilted petticoat*

Made 1 silk gown

Cut and made 1 sac for myself

Made double woollen dressing gown for D.

1 *pair of carpet-slippers for D.*

Made 4 towels

3 *large lined curtains. 3 small ditto.*

4 *pillow cases*

New collars & wristbands to 6 shirts

1 *night cap*

1 *pair of summer pantaloons*

Made a starred crib quilt, and quilted it; one fort-
   night's work
Spent 4 days collecting and sorting papers & pamphlets
   scattered by the fire
Mended 5 pair of drawers
Mended 10 pair of stockings
Cooked 360 dinners
Cooked 362 breakfasts
Swept & dusted sitting room & kitchen 350 times
Filled lamp 362 times
Swept & dusted chamber & stairs 40 times besides
   innumerable jobs too small to be mentioned
Preserved half a peck of barberries
Made 5 visits to aged women
Tended upon invalid friend two days
Made one day's visit to Medford and 3 visits to Bos-
   ton; 2 of them for one day, the other for two days
Made 7 calls upon neighbors
Cut and dried half a peck of dried apples

So great a number of chores would seem to have left
little time or energy for thinking on larger things. But
Maria's letters show that while her hands were never at
rest, neither was her mind. She kept one eye on the progress of the war on the battlefields, and the other on the
struggle shaping up in Congress over how to reconstruct
the South when the war would be over.

The final weeks of the war were thrilling. On the 31st of

January the Thirteenth Amendment to the Constitution, abolishing slavery in the United States, passed the House of Representatives. It was the sunrise of a new day for the Republic, the abolitionists felt. Now they were gathering the fruit of which they had planted the seed.

In Charleston, South Carolina, Garrison's son entered the captured city at the head of black troops, and in captured Richmond, Lincoln sent dispatches from Jeff Davis' house. A few days later, the President was dead by the assassin's bullet.

Looking back over the sweep of the years, Maria wondered to Whittier whether, if they could have foreseen what was to come, the abolitionists would have dared to fulfill the mission to which they were called. We would have known it was our *duty* to crush slavery, she said, but would we have had the *courage?*

Now, when victory was secure, she hoped the government would show itself magnanimous and merciful. She did not want the record to be blotted by revenge. "Through all this war, I have never had any feeling of hardness or hostility toward Southerners. The outrages they have committed are all chargeable upon the influence of their poisonous *system.*"

While she wanted justice to be tempered with mercy, she hoped the reins would be held with a very firm hand, "for any concession to these arrogant slaveholders will be supposed to be the result of our fear, and will be used for mischievous purposes." The slaveholders, she urged, must be left no power over loyal whites and emancipated blacks.

But as Andrew Johnson took over the murdered President's office, it quickly became plain that he was going to be very lenient with the Confederates. Before 1865 had closed, Southern state legislatures were adopting "Black Codes" which bound the freedmen to the land and virtually restored them to their old condition of bondage.

Maria was "disgusted with the mush of concession passing under the name of magnanimity. Both sides were *not* equal in right and it is wrong to say so," she insisted.

She asked why Robert E. Lee should be a gentleman at large while such of his subordinates as the keeper of notorious Andersonville prison camp, subject to Lee's orders, was hanged?

All distinctions between right and wrong are confounded, she said, when Lee is handled with velvet gloves because he is the lord of Arlington House. She regretted that the golden moment at Appomattox was lost. At that time of defeat, the rebels would have been glad to yield to any terms, without difficulty. But it was the country's misfortune to have men in power victimized by the old habit of fraternizing with slaveholders. "When they *should* have treated them as traitors, they were seized with a mania for treating them as unfortunate gentlemen."

Now, she pointed out, freedmen were being tortured and murdered in many places in the South, and in how few instances had retributive justice been done them!

President Johnson himself took no note of the atrocities and said he didn't believe a word of such reports. "I don't know what the poor freedmen think of their 'Moses,' but, if they knew enough to quote poetry, I should think they would say, 'Humane to *lords* and *ladies, Kings & counts,* Humane to such as we? Believe it not. The king, to do his *cousin* kindness, will canter over our bodies.'"

All summer long Maria was busy making *The Freedmen's Book*. It was an anthology of short biographies, poems, essays, and songs, all dealing with the Negro, and many of the selections by Negroes. Maria wanted to encourage, stimulate, and instruct the freedmen. "I am taking more pains with this book," she wrote Samuel May, "than if it were intended for young princes, or sprigs of what we call nobility."

She rewrote nearly every piece she found—doing a great many biographical sketches herself—in order to make everything very simple, clear, and condensed for inexperienced readers. Mixed in with the rest were four short pieces of her practical advice: how to care for animals, for children, and for health, and how to stand up for one's rights in the new condition of freedom.

She figured that to publish one edition of two thousand copies would cost about $1,200. With every hour she could snatch from household chores, she wrote articles for periodicals, in order to raise money to publish the book. But with all her working and managing she succeeded in laying up only $600. She was almost resigned to waiting another year or two to get the rest of the money when she saw a new reason to plunge ahead.

Everyone was debating whether freedmen should have suffrage. Wouldn't her book show what Negroes *had* done, and therefore *could* do? If she could get it out in a hurry, it might diminish prejudice among the whites and help win the freedmen the right to vote. "On that hinge I feel the safety of the Republic turns," she said.

Her feeling was confirmed by a letter she received from the Negro leader Frederick Douglass. "I have always read with grateful pleasure what you have from time to time written on the question of slavery," he wrote. "I am just now deeply engaged in the advocacy of suffrage for the whole colored people of the South. I see little advantage in emancipation without this. Unfriendly legislation by a state may undo all the friendly legislation by the Federal Government."

She went to the publishers, Ticknor & Fields. Would they risk publishing a book of such doubtful profit, if she would guarantee to buy $600 worth as soon as published? To her great relief they said yes, and offered to let her have that amount for the cost of paper, printing, and binding.

Her plan was to enlist as salesmen the teachers who had gone south to open the new schools for the freedmen. If any money came back to her, she would invest it in more books for them. And when they stopped buying the book, whatever money was left she would put into libraries for their use. In that way she hoped her $600 would do considerable good. (Her *Sunset* book, now out a year, had earned $1,000; she had put most of it into books, clothes, and tools for the freedmen.)

She was not content to prepare *The Freedmen's Book*. She would promote it, too. She wrote a short circular for the press, telling what the book was about and what she hoped it would do. She suggested that Ticknor & Fields send it, together with review copies, to several papers in New York and Boston.

After the book came out, Maria found wages were so very low among the freedmen—when they were paid at all—that few could afford the price. In the next few years she spent another $1,200 of her own money to have the book given away by the Freedmen's Aid Society.

17 &c Prejudice and Principles

The war had been won. Lincoln had signed the Emancipation Proclamation. The Thirteenth Amendment to the Constitution, adopted in 1865, had confirmed the Negro's freedom. The Fourteenth, guaranteeing his rights as a citizen, had just been passed by Congress. But these were documents, words, promises. In the cities, on the farms, could black people stand erect? Did they know equality?

"I fought against *slavery* till I saw it go down in the Red Sea," Maria said. "Now I want to do something to undermine *prejudice.*" There was such a universal passion for novels, what better way to show the evil stamp slavery had put on American life than through a good story?

Maria had the nucleus of a plot in mind. In the middle of the war she had mentioned her idea to Sarah Shaw, who was so taken with it she gave Maria a handsome desk and begged her to write the story on it. Three or four chapters unwound, but Maria got discouraged; a sustained effort was hard in the midst of suffering. The fragment stayed in a drawer until James Fields pressed her to write a novel his *Atlantic Monthly* could serialize. For a year and a half Maria's head seethed with the book. She plotted a large framework for it and carefully laid all the joints so that it would come out right in every particular. It cost her many a headache and many a wakeful hour. When it was finished, Fields was so taken with it he wanted to publish it at once as a novel; she would make more by it that way, he said.

The Romance of the Republic appeared in 1867. It was a story of slavery days, with two lovely quadroon sisters as the heroines. Although Maria had never visited the deep South, she had learned enough about it to give it true coloring. Her characters were a cross section of society, both North and South, and she put them through every conceivable twist of plot to show the reader how slavery influenced national life in all its aspects.

Maria watched anxiously for the public response. She had never cared so much about the success of any of her books. It is "the Benjamin of my family, the child of my old age," she said. But the book brought her disappointment and even humiliation. "I did not form any *great* calculations upon it," she confided to Louisa Loring, "but I did please myself with the idea that I had five or six friends who would be glad to see that my mind had not lost all its freshness by years, and solitude, and uncongenial occupations."

One or two friends wrote that the book proved she was "still in the flower of her age," but she heard so few, and such faint, echoes from the book that she feared it was a failure. Too many friends she sent the book said simply "Thank you," and some said nothing at all.

"All this has had a very depressing effect upon me," she told Louisa. "When I had completed the book, I felt as if I could write another and a better novel, and was full of earnestness to set about it, but the apathy of my friends took all the life out of me, and has made me feel as if I never wanted to put pen to paper again."

Some critics thought her plot ingenious and the characters lively, but others said the story was too romantic and the twists of plot incredible. Against this charge she stoutly defended herself: "There is nothing imagined that might not very naturally have happened, under the laws, customs, and opinions then existing." She proved to her friends that many incidents were woven into the fiction and named the real people upon whom many of her characters were modeled. She had made the mistake many a writer makes when he assumes that just because his material is taken from real life, it will inevitably appear real to his readers.

Although she lacked the art to convince her audience through fiction, her power to marshal facts in behalf of a cause was as great as ever. And soon she was putting it to use again.

While the war against slavery was being won by Lincoln's armies, out in the West another war for human freedom was being lost—almost unnoticed. Mining companies, railroads, and homesteading veterans were shoving the Indians off their lands. The tribes fought back, but too much power was massed against them. In Colorado the bitter conflict lasted until a massacre of 450 Indians forced the tribes to submit. United States troops warred against Cheyenne, Arapaho, Apache, Navaho, and Sioux—one after the other they were chased from place to place and pushed into barren corners.

Near the close of the Civil War a congressional committee was appointed to study the condition of the Indian tribes. Out of its hearings came a peace commission which sought to end the Indian wars and formulate a permanent Indian policy.

Maria studied the Peace Commission's report. Her concern for the Indians was as strong as when she had written *Hobomok* and *The First Settlers of New England* almost forty years earlier. With their plight pressing again for government attention, she thought the commission's report a good occasion to publish another appeal to the nation's conscience.

She wished to heaven the Indians had education and

newspapers to tell their side of the story. They were driven to desperation by starvation and embittered by promises that were never fulfilled. But you could hardly get a glimpse of the real facts from what the press published. In 1868 she issued *An Appeal for the Indians*.

Why must force always be used to settle issues, Maria asked her readers. "We are so long indulged in feelings of pride and contempt toward those whom we are pleased to call 'the subject races' that we have actually become incapable of judging them with any tolerable degree of candor or common sense."

Religion, too, she blamed for the way the Indians were treated. Christian nations dealing with peoples of other faiths and lesser power, she wrote, never act on the same moral principles as those by which they themselves expect to be treated.

The commission recommended that the Indians be placed on reservations under a governor with a salary large enough to place him above temptation. But Maria foresaw that no salary would prevent prejudiced whites from being unfair and corrupt in such a situation.

She found the old curse of white superiority at work again when the commission condemned the "barbarous dialect" of the Indians and insisted the Indian children be taught only in the English language. She urged instead that their books be printed in their own tongue, side by side with English translations, and using the best of their own traditions and history.

Her advice was sound, but ignored. The government's policy led only to more conflict and bloodier massacres. Maria began to feel it was almost impossible to convince politicians that it is not "visionary" to be guided by decent principles in public affairs. It's their idea, she said, that the greater the double-dealing, the greater the statesmanship.

But she never quite gave up. She was happy to hear that Senator Sumner had passed on to General Sherman —now in charge of Indian affairs—her letters about the Indians. "If I can have the least bit of influence in changing the policy toward those much-abused tribes, it will be something worth living for . . . . It is a comfort to me to think that, however much wrong I may have done, I have never written anything that can do any harm."

As the country settled into peacetime living, friends tried to persuade Maria and David to move into Boston or to New York, where they might find more congenial company and livelier pursuits. Maria confessed that she was sometimes restless in Wayland. But the Childs had no means to do any better. Her income—David had none —fell short of $800 a year. Out of it she paid $50 annually to help support an invalid sister of David's, and taxes took another $170. That left about $550 for food, clothing, perpetually recurring repairs, replenishing furniture, fuel, lamplight, medicines, stage and train fares, etc. Here in Wayland they could have every necessity but how could she mix with society without running into debt? Rely more on your pen, her friends suggested; but at her age, she answered, it might fail her at any moment. Instead of trying to live on earnings from her writing, which averaged $300 to $400 a year, she used this income only as a benevolent fund, chiefly for the freedmen. She gave $50 to the antislavery society in 1868, and one member noted that "few households in the country contributed on a scale so very liberal, in proportion to their means." Once, when Frank Shaw sent her $200 as a gift just after her house had burned, she returned it because, she said, others needed it more. Another time, she sent Wendell Phillips $100 for the freedmen, but he returned it, saying he didn't think she could afford to give so much now. Let me think it over, she replied. The next day she sent him $200. She was amused to cite her few extravagances: $18.02 spent in one year for clothing, and 50 cents for entertainment. Books and pictures she almost never bought, except now and then for a gift to a child. Her greatest extravagance in years was to spend $7.00 for a book on the science of language as a birthday present for David.

As for self-adornment—in 1866 she mentioned in a letter that she had been contemplating for twelve years the purchase of an elegant bonnet, but hadn't been able to work herself up to buying it. Her ancient bonnet—to which she clung forever, it seemed—became a landmark at public meetings. She had to promise several people that she would call on them whenever she got a fashionable one. One friend heard a rumor that Maria had actually acquired a new hat, but when she wrote to ask about it, Maria replied that repairs on the old cistern had proved too expensive and the old bonnet would have to do a bit longer. "Such an old-fashioned heap as I am you never saw," she added. "I beat Elizabeth Peabody, out and out. If Barnum should get sight of me, I am afraid he would be after me for his travelling museum."

She was something of a celebrity, of course: an old-time abolitionist who had lived on into the postwar years and whose oddities and humors were gossip for all. One story goes that a stranger meeting her in a stagecoach inquired, "Who is that woman who dresses like a peasant and speaks like a scholar?" People asked for her picture and her autograph in such numbers that she sat for a Boston photographer and let him sell prints at forty-two cents each. But she didn't think much of such popularity. "I daresay General Tom Thumb is inundated with such requests," she remarked.

The papers ran biographical sketches of her now and then, but she wasn't impressed. "The same honor befalls hundreds below the level of mediocrity," she said. "I think few things are more inconvenient and disagreeable than being a 'small' lion. One loses the advantage of complete obscurity without attaining to the advantages of great fame. If what I have written has been the means of doing any good in the world, I am thankful; but as for personal gratification in receiving, as a lion, what you call 'the homage of smaller animals,' I have none. All I want is to be left in peace to do quietly the work which my hands find to do."

Part of growing old was seeing her friends die all about her. When Ellis Loring died after she had seen him well only a week before, it gave her such a shock she could never leave a friend afterward without feeling it might be for the last time. Her brother Convers had died during the war; now she began numbering the few friends who were left.

David, nearly eight years her senior, was her constant care. His health was so precarious that any change of routine brought on serious illness. He busied himself digging in the garden and chopping in the woodlot. His spirits were lively and cheerful as long as he could plan "improvements." At seventy-five he was still able to cut four cartloads of wood between morning and twilight. The one mission Maria felt she had left to perform was to make his old age as comfortable and happy as she could.

To that end, she said, "I read only 'chipper' books. I hang prisms in my windows to fill the room with rainbows; I gaze at all the bright pictures in shop windows; I cultivate the gayest flowers; I seek cheerfulness in every possible way."

Still, she never shut her eyes to what was going on in her world. She was glad to see President Johnson impeached, but regretted it was not done on the more proper ground of the mess he had tried to make of Reconstruction. She watched the vast new territories of the West open up and lamented that she no longer knew the geography of her own country. She went strong for General Grant's presidential race, giving money and rounding up votes, although she didn't think he'd ever shown the slightest interest in the Negro people. What she feared more than his apathy was that if the Democrats returned to power they would destroy Reconstruction and set back the Negroes. At least, she said, a simple, unpretending man like Grant might be counted on to give equal justice to all classes of people.

About war, she said that "as a mere matter of common sense, it is the most absurd thing imaginable. It is assumed that war settles questions of right, but the plain truth is, that nothing is ever settled by physical force. The settling has to be done afterward, by mutual treaties and laws; and it would be wiser, and cheaper, and far more kindly to settle disputes in *that* way, with the omission of the monstrous prelude of blowing out one another's brains."

The movement for woman's suffrage began gaining momentum in the 1870's and Maria gave it her support. Now, with slavery dead, it was the most important of all questions to her. And for reasons somewhat special. Yes, she said, a woman's condition and character would be immeasurably improved by habits of thinking and acting on matters of grave responsibility. But *men* would be still more benefited by the change. "No domestic happiness is to be compared with that which results from the wife's capacity to sympathize with all the pursuits of her husband, whether in art, science, literature, business, or politics." Men don't realize what they lose by having wives, daughters, and sisters who are mere domestic drudges or dolls of fashion.

To the charge that most women were not asking for any change in their status, she replied that it merely proved they were the unthinking slaves of custom. One of the worst results of subjugation was that it made its victims so used to their condition that they saw no need of change. It takes the rare and fiery few to rouse the sleepers, she said, concluding one message to women with the line, "Yours for the unshackled exercise of every faculty by every human being."

18 ⛓ Tongue of Flame

The last years of quiet companionship glided away. "We are like two old children," Maria said: "We keep young in our feelings, as interested as ever in the birds and the wild flowers." As he neared eighty David became so disabled by rheumatism Maria didn't dare leave him alone lest he burn or scald himself. She could not go outside her gate for months at a time. In his last months he grew feebler, but he bore his suffering patiently, his mind never clouding nor his spirit failing. On a September midnight in 1874, he died peacefully in Maria's arms.

She was so thankful she had been able to take care of him to the last, but no tongue could tell how desolate his going left her. A month later they would have celebrated their forty-fifth wedding anniversary. She felt like a hungry child lost in a dark wood. In November her best and most loyal friends, the Shaws, brought her to their Staten Island home for a long visit. She wouldn't cross the harbor into New York. Daily she walked along the beach, thinking how much the human heart could go through and still live on. In the winter, she was back in her lonely house again, despairing, but "still hoping to be of use in the world, in some way."

All her friends tried to help her, asking her to stay with them, seeking to take her out, worrying about how she would get along alone. After David's death, she spent her last winters in Boston. It was a great desert to her. She walked the streets without meeting a single familiar face, where once she had encountered warm handclasps at every corner. The rest of the year she was at Wayland, living very much to herself, except for trying to help neighbors or strangers whenever she could. There was the husband of the woman who washed and scoured for her for many years. He drank up all his wages, beat his wife, and finally set fire to his employer's barn, destroying the cattle. When he came out of jail two years later, his eyes had such a beseeching look, as if his soul were hungry for a friend, that Maria promised to give him work if he would stay sober. He kept his promise, and so did she, even leaving him fifty dollars a year in her will so long as he should stay away from liquor.

One after the other she took three unwed mothers in to live with her for months at a time, hoping to get them started right again in a cold world. This experiment didn't work, however; they always fell again, she said, after leaving her home to try to make a living outside. They were among the host of forlorn beings who go through life with souls perishing for want of somebody to love them and somebody to love, their characters so blighted by neglect and hardened by harshness.

In 1879 she was working to get the legislature to adopt more humane laws in behalf of people accused of insanity. A little later, when Chinese immigrants were being vilified and mobbed in California, she spoke out against the attempt to exclude them from the country. "We have no right to put up a barrier against any class of people who obey the laws," she said. "It violates the principles of our government, and the principles of humanity."

When Reconstruction was ended in the South by the compromise between the Republicans and Democrats which put Hayes in the White House, Maria was appalled at how defenseless the freedmen were left. To emancipate the Negroes and leave them to the tender mercies of their ex-masters was "the most wicked and cruel thing a government ever did," she said.

Soon thousands of Negroes from the deep South were fleeing to the North and West, seeking a living away from the miseries of sharecropping and the terrors of mobs.

Southerners tried to hold back the ebbing tide of labor but the exodus went on. "Thank God that safety valve is open!" Maria wrote.

In her last July, Maria wrote a warm letter to her old abolitionist friend Theodore Weld, recalling the early antislavery days as very sacred to her. "The 'Holy' Spirit *did* actually descend upon men and women in tongues of flame," she said. "Mortals were never more sublimely forgetful of self . . . . Ah, my friend, that is the only *true* church organization, when heads and hearts unite in working for the welfare of the human race . . . . I look back lovingly upon those days."

She had no patience with a friend who said that maybe the Negroes were better off in slavery. "Even in my most despairing moods, I will not admit *that,*" Maria replied. "Notwithstanding the miserable blunders of our government, and the abominable knavery of politicians, there *has* been a great gain. They cannot be bought and sold in the market; they can emigrate; and we have made no contract to send them back. Best of all, there is now a possible *basis* for the salutary education of both races, and under the old system there *was* no such possibility."

No matter how many dangers or how much suffering is involved in every effort to better our world, we can only follow patiently and fearlessly every principle which we clearly see is true, she added.

As for those who worry about time-serving and self-seeking leaders, she said: "All great revolutions and reformations would look mean and meager if examined in detail as they occurred at the time . . . . Still more wonderful is it to observe what poor, mean cattle God yokes to the car of progress, and makes them draw in a direction they are striving to avoid . . . . The details are often ludicrous exhibitions of human inconsistency and selfishness, but the result is sublime . . . ."

In the fall of 1880, rheumatism bothered Maria, and she had to stay in bed for some time. Hating the thought of outliving her usefulness, she wrote a friend, "The only strong wish I have is to retain my faculties to the last, and slip away quietly out of this world, so as not to make anybody much trouble."

With that in mind, she told friends she wanted a simple burial, with no flowers, and to lie in the same ground with colored people.

"Oh, but you'll be buried in Mount Auburn!" they said.

"No," she replied, "I will not; it would be too near the Boston aristocracy."

On the morning of October 20, 1880, her heart failed her, and she died quietly, at the age of seventy-eight. Three days later the services were held in her house, with many old friends present. The minister was the village clergyman. Then Wendell Phillips spoke. "She was ready to die for a principle and starve for an idea, nor think to claim any merit for it," he said. As the casket was being taken from the house, a flock of blackbirds flew up and perched on Maria's willow and elm, filling the air with song. The old farmers she had known as neighbors bore her through the vivid leaves, between rows of thick evergreens, and put her in the earth. Nearby were the graves of two slaves.

"I sweep dead leaves out of paths and dust mirrors," she said once.

Afterword

All the quotations in this book are taken from authentic records. Thoughts put into Maria's head are never invented, but reconstructed from passages in her own letters or other writings. Nor are any incidents in her story imagined, except for the opening chapter, where I have taken the liberty of making Maria and her father participants in the episode of the runaway slave Caesar. That event actually occurred at that time, and it seems likely that in so small a town the family of Maria's abolitionist father might well have found itself in the middle of the excitement.

Selected Bibliography

Letters, notes, scrapbooks, and other unpublished materials of Lydia Maria Child were examined in or obtained from the following sources:

The American Antiquarian Society.

Boston Public Library. Lydia Maria Child Correspondence, Child Papers, Garrison Papers, Weston Papers, Phelps Papers.

Department of Rare Books, Cornell University Library. Slavery and Abolition Collection.

Friends Historical Library of Swarthmore College.

The Houghton Library, Library of Harvard University.

Manuscript Division, New York Public Library. Bryant-Godwin Collection, Greeley Papers, and Personal Miscellaneous Papers.

Massachusetts Historical Society.

New York Historical Society.

The Ohio Historical Society. Giddings Papers.

William L. Clements Library, The University of Michigan. Weld Papers and Miscellaneous Manuscripts.

The Women's Archives, Radcliffe College. Loring Papers and the Alma Lutz Collection.

Yale University Library.

Works by Lydia Maria Child

The following books and pamphlets by Mrs. Child are listed in order of their publication dates. The newspaper and magazine articles by Mrs. Child are too numerous to include here.

Hobomok; a Tale of Early Times. Boston, 1824.

The Rebels; or, Boston before the Revolution. Boston, 1825.

The Juvenile Miscellany. 1826–1834.

The Juvenile Souvenir. Boston, 1828.

The First Settlers of New England; or, Conquest of the Pequods, Narragansets, and Pokanokets. As related by a mother to her children. Boston, 1829.

The Frugal Housewife. Boston, 1830.

The Mother's Book. Boston, 1831.

The Girl's Own Book. Boston, 1831.

The Coronal; a Collection of Miscellaneous Pieces, Written at Various Times. Boston, 1831.

The Ladies Library

    Vol. I. Biographies of Lady Russell and Madame Guion. Boston, 1832.

    Vol. II. Biographies of Madame de Stael and Madame Roland. Boston, 1832.

    Vol. III. Biographies of Good Wives. Boston, 1833.

Vol. IV.-V. *History of the Condition of Women in Various Ages and Nations.* New York, 1835.

An Appeal in Behalf of that Class of Americans called Africans. Boston, 1833.

The Oasis. Boston, 1834.

An Anti-Slavery Catechism. Newburyport, 1836.

The Evils of Slavery and the Cure of Slavery. The first proved by the opinions of Southerners themselves; the last shown by historical evidence. Newburyport, 1836.

Philothea: a Romance. Boston, 1836.

The Family Nurse. Boston, 1837.

Authentic Narratives of American Slavery. Newburyport, 1838.

Rose Marian and the Flower Fairies. 1839.

"The Preaching of Whitefield," in *Boston Book,* 1841.

The Anti-Slavery Almanac. New York, 1843.

Letters from New York, First Series. New York, 1843.

Flowers for Children, First and Second Series. New York, 1844.

Letters from New York, Second Series. New York, 1845.

Fact and Fiction. New York, 1846.

Flowers for Children, Third Series. New York, 1846.

Rainbows for Children. New York, 1848.

Isaac T. Hopper; a True Life. Boston, 1853.

New Flowers for Children. 1855.

The Progress of Religious Ideas through Successive Ages. 3 vols. New York, 1855.

Autumnal Leaves: Tales and Sketches in Prose and Rhyme. New York, 1856.

Correspondence between Lydia Maria Child, Governor Wise and Mrs. Mason. Boston, 1860.

The Duty of Disobedience to the Fugitive Slave Act. An Appeal to the Legislators of Massachusetts. Boston, 1860.

The Patriarchal Institution, Described by Members of its Own Family. New York, 1860.

The Right Way, the Safe Way, Proved by Emancipation in the West Indies and Elsewhere. New York, 1860.

Incidents in the Life of a Slave Girl. (ed.). Boston, 1861.

Looking Toward Sunset. From Sources Old and New, Original and Selected. Boston, 1864.

The Freedmen's Book. Boston, 1865.

A Romance of the Republic. Boston, 1867.

An Appeal for the Indians. New York (1868?).

Children of Mt. Ida. New York, 1871.

Aspirations of the World. Boston, 1878.

Works on Lydia Maria Child

Baer, Helene G. *The Heart Is Like Heaven: The Life of Lydia Maria Child.* Philadelphia, 1964.

——. "Mrs. Child and Miss Fuller," *New England Quarterly,* XXVI (June, 1953), 249–253.

Barnes, James A. (ed.). "Letters of Lydia Maria Child to

George W. Julian: 1862–1878," *Indiana Magazine of History* (March, 1930), 46–60.

Beach, Seth C. *Daughters of the Puritans*. Boston, 1905.

Curtis, George T. "Reminiscences of N. P. Willis and Lydia Maria Child," *Harpers Magazine*, LXXXI (October, 1890), 717–720.

Edwards, Herbert. "Frugal Housewife," *New England Quarterly* (June, 1953), 243–249.

Higginson, Thomas Wentworth. "Lydia Maria Child," *Contemporaries*, Boston, 1899. 108–141.

Hudson, A. S. "The Home of Lydia Maria Child," *New England Magazine* (June, 1890), 402–414.

Lamberton, Berenice G. *A Biography of Lydia Maria Child*. Unpublished doctoral dissertation, University of Maryland, 1953. (Microfilm in library of Mrs. Arthur C. Holden.)

"Letters of Wendell Phillips to Lydia Maria Child," *New England Magazine* (February, 1892).

Streeter, Robert E. "Mrs. Child's *Philothea*—a Transcendental Novel?" *New England Quarterly* (December, 1943).

Taylor, Lloyd C., Jr. *An Interpretative Study of Lydia Maria Child*. Unpublished doctoral dissertation, Lehigh University, 1956. (Microfilm, New York Public Library.)

———. "Lydia Maria Child: Biographer," *New England Quarterly* (June, 1961).

———. "Lydia Maria Child and the Indians," *Boston Public Library Quarterly* (January, 1960).

Ware, Ethel K. "Lydia Maria Child and Anti-Slavery," *Boston Public Library Bulletin* (October, 1951, and January, 1952).

Weld, T. D., A. G. Weld, and Sarah Grimke. *Letters . . . 1822–1844.* New York: Dwight L. Dumond and Gilbert H. Barnes, 1934. (Letters from Lydia Maria Child in V. II on pp. 692–695, 702–705, 724–732, 734–736.)

Background

Brooks, Charles, and James M. Usher. *History of the Town of Medford.* Boston, 1886.

Brooks, Van Wyck. *The Flowering of New England.* New York, 1936.

———. *The World of Washington Irving.* New York, 1944.

Brown, Arthur W. *Always Young for Liberty: A Biography of William Ellery Channing.* Syracuse, 1956.

Buckmaster, Henrietta. *Let My People Go.* New York, 1941.

Case of the Slave Child, Med. Boston, 1836.

Chadwick, John W. (ed.). *A Life for Liberty: Anti-Slavery and Other Letters of Sallie Holley.* New York, 1899.

Commager, Henry Steele. *Theodore Parker.* Boston, 1937.

Cutting, Alfred. *Old Time Wayland.* Wayland, 1926.

Donald, David. *Charles Sumner and the Coming of the Civil War*. New York, 1960.

Filler, Louis. *The Crusade Against Slavery*. New York, 1960.

Foner, Philip. *Business and Slavery*. New York, 1941.

Franklin, John Hope. *Reconstruction After the Civil War*. Ann Arbor, 1960.

———. *From Slavery to Freedom*. New York, 1947.

Frothingham, O. B. *Transcendentalism in New England*. 1876.

———. *Theodore Parker*. New York, 1886.

Hallowell, A. D. *James and Lucretia Mott, Life and Letters*. Boston, 1884.

Hudson, Frederic. *Journalism in the United States: 1690–1872*. New York, 1873.

Johnson, Oliver. *William Lloyd Garrison and His Times*. Boston, 1880.

Korngold, Ralph. *Two Friends of Man*. Boston, 1950.

Litwack, Leon F. *North of Slavery*. Chicago, 1961.

May, Samuel J. *Recollections of Our Anti-Slavery Conflict*. Boston, 1869.

Merrill, Walter M. *Against Wind and Tide: A Biography of William Lloyd Garrison*. Cambridge, 1963.

Mott, Frank Luther. *American Journalism*. New York, 1950.

Nichols, Thomas L. *Forty Years of American Life: 1821–1861*. New York, 1937.

Nye, Russel B. *Fettered Freedom*. East Lansing, 1949.

Pickard, Samuel T. *Life and Letters of John Greenleaf Whittier*. 2 vols. Boston, 1894.

Quincy, Josiah. *Figures of the Past*. Boston, 1883.

Right and Wrong in Boston. Boston, 1837.

Sherwin, Oscar. *Prophet of Liberty: The Life and Times of Wendell Phillips*. New York, 1958.

Stearns, Bertha-Monica. "Reform Periodicals and Female Reformers, 1830–1860." *American Historical Review*, V. XXXVII, pp. 678–699.

Stearns, Frank Preston. *The Life and Public Services of George Luther Stearns*. Philadelphia, 1907.

Ticknor, George. *Life, Letters and Journals*. 2 vols. Boston, 1880.

Tyler, Alice Felt. *Freedom's Ferment*. Minneapolis, 1944.

Villard, Oswald Garrison. *John Brown*. Boston, 1910.

Wilson, James. *A Memorial History of the City of New York*, 4 vols. New York, 1892–1893.

Files of *The Liberator* and the *National Anti-Slavery Standard* were frequently referred to for day-to-day developments in the abolitionist movement as well as for pieces by or about Lydia Maria Child.

Index

About the Author

MILTON MELTZER, distinguished biographer and historian, is the author of more than seventy books for young people and adults. Born in Worcester, Massachusetts, and educated at Columbia University, he worked for the WPA Federal Theater Project and then served in the Air Force in World War II. He has edited and written for newspapers, magazines, radio, TV, and films.

Among the many honors for his books are five nominations for the National Book Award, as well as the Christopher, Jane Addams, Carter G. Woodson, Jefferson Cup, Washington Book Guild, Olive Branch, and Golden Kite awards. The Lydia Maria Child life was one of the earliest among his eighteen biographies. Years later he collected and edited the complete letters of Mrs. Child, who was not only a pioneer abolitionist and advocate of women's rights but a novelist, historian, newspaper editor, columnist, author of books on household management and child care, and publisher of one of the earliest magazines for children.

Mr. Meltzer and his wife live in New York City. They have two daughters and a grandson. Mr. Meltzer is a member of the Author's Guild.